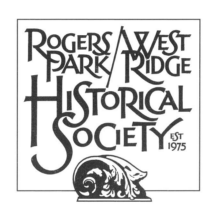

D1558628

Neighborhoods Within Neighborhoods
Twentieth Century Life on
Chicago's Far North Side

by Neal Samors and Michael Williams with Mary Jo Doyle

Foreword by Dan Miller Essays by Ira Berkow, Hugh Downs,
Steve Friedman, and Congresswoman Jan Schakowsky

Rogers Park/West Ridge Historical Society

Published in the United States of America in 2002 by the
Rogers Park/West Ridge Historical Society.

© 2002 by the Rogers Park/West Ridge Historical Society.

First printing: February, 2002.

Edited by Neal Samors, Michael Williams, Mary Jo Doyle, Sue Sosin
and Marcee Williams.

Produced by James B. Kirkpatrick of Kirk's Computer Service.

Book design by Michael Williams.

Printed in Canada by Friesens Corporation.

ISBN: 0-9716842-0-0 - soft cover

Front cover: Midnight Show at the Ridge Theatre, c.1945. Photograph by
Henry Green. (Courtesy of the Chicago Historical Society, ICHi 32263.)

Back cover: Mayor Richard J. Daley with Mel Thillens, Sr. at Thillens Stadium,
c.1960.

Frontispiece: Howard Theatre Bond Booth, 1944. Photograph by Henry Green.
(Courtesy of the Chicago Historical Society, ICHi 25620.)

For more information on the Rogers Park/West Ridge Historical Society,
contact us at:
Phone: (773) 764-4078 or 4079
Fax: (773) 764-2824
Website: www.rpwrhs.org
E-mail: rpwrhs@aol.com

Contents

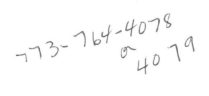

Acknowledgments

We want to express our sincere gratitude for the generous financial contributions received from Jack and Donna Price Greenberg and the McDonald's Foundation, the Brach Foundation, Devon Bank, John R. Conrad and the S&C Electric Company and Arthur C. Nielsen, Jr. Their support of this project, and of the Rogers Park/West Ridge Historical Society, was key to funding the printing of this book. Also, a special thank you to Neil Hartigan for his support and encouragement in raising funds for the printing of this book.

Also, we want to offer very special appreciation to the authors of the guest essays in this publication who took time from very busy schedules to compile their memories and recollections of experiences living in the neighborhoods, as well as their perceptions of what defines a "neighborhood," both today and throughout the twentieth century.

Journalist Ira Berkow, broadcaster Hugh Downs, television producer Steve Friedman, journalist Daniel J. Miller, and U.S. Congresswoman Janice Danoff Schakowsky graciously contributed those essays.

The authors want to express our thanks to the numerous individuals and organizations that worked with us to make their photograph collections available for this book. They include Russell Lewis of the Chicago Historical Society, Julia Bachrach and Robert Middaugh of the Chicago Park District, Jeff Stern of the Chicago Transit Authority, Jerry Austiff of the Metropolitan Water Reclamation District, Jack Bess of the Lerner Newspapers, Dan Miller of the *Chicago Sun-Times*, Bro. Michael J. Grace, S.J. of Loyola University, Sr. Ann Ida Gannon and Valerie Brown of Mundelein College, Julie Satzik and Rebecca Hartman of the Archdiocese of Chicago, Jeannette Katz of

Congregation B'nai Zion, Sr. Vivian Ivantic of St. Scholastica Academy, Richard Sklenar of the Theatre Historical Society of America, Marie Roti of St. Ignatius Church, Sullivan High School and the staff of the Harold Washington Branch of the Chicago Public Library.

Our deep appreciation and acknowledgment to the following individuals whose oral histories provided the authors with the rich details concerning memories of what life was like during their years in the Rogers Park and West Ridge neighborhoods during the twentieth century. Their stories are poignant, vibrant and humorous, and add much flavor to this book.

Joan Wester Anderson, David Beck, Gary Berg, Shelly Lang Berger, Ira Berkow, Arthur Berman, Bob Berman, Dorothy Katz Berez, Dr. Ira Bernstein, Dr. Sidney Bild, Alvin Blackman, Cookie Brandt, Tim Cavey,

Steve Chernof, Marcia Froelke Coburn, Bobbi Rosenthal Cohen, Roger Cooper, Betty Serlin Covici, Cameron Dall, Bob Dauber, Ruth Levin Dauber, Abdulaziz Daya, Eileen Deegan, Marshall Dermer, Joan Reiter Downing, Hugh Downs and Mary Jo Behrendt Doyle.

Joseph Epstein, Sondra Fargo, Bobbi Levin Feinstein, Dorothy Dubrovsky Fields, Howard Fink, Judy Karpen Flapan, Steve Friedman, Sr. Ann Ida Gannon, Gail Gordon, Donna Price Greenberg, Shecky Greene, John Grigsby, Alan Gruenwald, Andy Halpern, Neil Hartigan, Clarence Hess, Gladys Van Iderstine Hoagland, Frank Hogan, Katy Hogan, Janie Friedman Isackson, Sr. Vivian Ivantic, Glenn Jacobs, Michael James, Bill Jauss and Mitch Joseph.

Irwin Kanefsky, Shari Phillips Kanefsky, Jeannette Katz, James Kirkpatrick, Rick Kogan, Brian Kozin, Carl LaMell, Gary Landau, Marsha Schwartz Landau, Richard Lang, Ian Levin, Joseph Levinson, Dale Lichtenstein, Barbara Cherney Mackevich, Edward Margolis, Norman Mark, Jackie Morrell McNicol, Ron Menaker, Dan Miller, Henry Miller, Lillian Minkus, Ed Mogul, Bill Nellis, Guadelupe Sanchez Ochoa, Herschel Oliff and David Orr.

Don Pardieck, Dr. Norman Poteshman, Nancy Goldman Rae, Shelly Raffel, Harold Ramis, Susan Rosenberg RoAne, Betty Major Rose, Norman Ross, Judy Schwade Rozner, Janice Danoff Schakowsky,

Howard Schein, David Schultz, Gordon Segal, Janet Schwade Seichelman, Carole Sensendorf, Gert Sensendorf, Marilyn Sensendorf, Eric Sheinin, Burt Sherman, Charles "Corky" Sherman, Ruth Aaronson Sherman, Marshal Shifrin, Lynne Ressman Simon-Lodwick, Scott Simon, Betsy Siegel Sinclair, Sue Sosin and John Staerk.

Ray Thill, Joan Berets Tiersky, Scott Turow, Betty Toben Warden, Joel Weisman, Jerry Wester, Marcee McGinnis Williams, Linda Holdman Wine, Marilyn Woitel, Bruce Wolf, Nancy Bild Wolf, Gena Martinez Zalenka, Michael Zelmar and Linda Lanoff Zimmerman.

Sue Sosin, Marcee Williams and Mary Jo Doyle earn the authors' deep gratitude for their editorial support in the completion of this publication. James Kirkpatrick, Society advisor and computer consultant, worked with the authors in the design and layout of this book and deserves special recognition. Member Sally Kirkpatrick assisted with the final proofreading. A very special thanks to the members of the board of the Rogers Park/ West Ridge Historical Society, including Roy Alexander, Mary Borke, Ellen Eslinger, Laurene Huffman, Don Kumkoski, Sue Sosin, Marcee Williams, and executive director, Mary Jo Doyle, for their continual support and encouragement in the completion of this project.

Foreword
by Dan Miller

It's easy to describe a Chicago neighborhood: It's located between these streets and those. It has this many houses, shops, churches, schools and parks, and the people who live there fit under this bell curve.

But it is definitely a stingy way to describe something as complex and as elegant as a Chicago neighborhood. In our city, a neighborhood is an emotion, the mere mention of which can summon memories that make the hair on the back of your neck stand up and constrict your throat ever so slightly. A Chicago neighborhood is the repository of personal experience and civic history, the portal where we first entered the city or where we grew up. It's where we made our best friends, lived with our families, and buried our dead. It's where we went to school, shopped, worked, and marched off to war. It's the place we returned to at the end of a day or a life, glad to be home.

Each individual also has defined his or her own neighborhood by very personal parameters. In childhood, a neighborhood may have been just one, two or several blocks long and wide, with very specific streets and intersections that usually limited broader exploration. During one's early years, the neighborhood usually included some stores and restaurants, a school, a religious institution, a movie theater, alleys, empty lots, parks and beaches. As one grew older, the boundaries of the neighborhood usually expanded to include more places and things to do, and one's circle of acquaintances and neighbors also sequentially increased. Greater opportunities to explore the wider city would present themselves through public transportation and family automobiles.

The memories of many events linger in the neighborhood, caught in the branches of the trees and in the mist along the Lake Michigan shore. They become part of our neighborhood as surely as its streets and light poles. The word neighborhood evokes shared experiences among friends and family, and dreams put aside. It's an ambidextrous word: it fits as neatly in the past -- "the old neighborhood" and "Mom and Dad's neighborhood" -- as it does in the present -- "this is my neighborhood."

Chicago's neighborhoods are like a patchwork quilt, Mayor Richard J. Daley was fond of saying. Each patch is different and distinct, but when they are "sewn" together, they make a beautiful whole. This book celebrates two of these neighborhoods, Rogers Park and West Ridge, and their six micro-neighborhoods -- Loyola, Morse, Howard, Ridge, West Rogers Park and North Town. They are sewn together along Ridge Avenue, and in their histories and current activities they illustrate how a patchwork quilt like Chicago is made.

Waves of immigrants -- from other parts of the United States and from foreign lands -- washed over Rogers Park and West Ridge, carving out residential enclaves and commercial plateaus from the lake to Kedzie and from Bryn Mawr to Howard. The kinds of homes and commerce in our neighborhood have changed over the generations, but not where they are located. Small farmhouses and shacks have given way to bungalows and million-dollar town-homes, while turkey and cabbage farmers have surrendered their acreage to car dealerships, restaurants and retailers. African-Americans, Koreans, Indians, Pakistanis, and Russians have joined Irish, Scots, Germans and Poles.

What is astonishing about Rogers Park and West Ridge, and their micro-neighborhoods, and what makes them and Chicago's other community areas crucial to the city itself, is that no one decreed that they should exist as they do. But as newcomers entered the neighborhood, they saw the success of their neighbors as a way to achieve their own goals of political and social stability, material well-being, safety and freedom. As separate and distinct as patches in a quilt, but sewn together by a common thread. Rogers Park and West Ridge embody respect for the rights and freedoms of neighbors, substituting joint action and cooperation for enmity and conflict.

This is what a neighborhood is. And what makes Chicago great. It has been a city of neighborhoods that emerged independently, not as a triumph over the diversity of the people or the incumbents and the newcomers, but as the result of joint action and cooperation among free individuals: neighbors making common cause to create and preserve a place called home.

Dan Miller is the Business Editor of the <u>Chicago Sun-Times</u>. He formerly worked for the <u>Chicago Daily News</u> and served as chairman of the Illinois Commerce Commission.

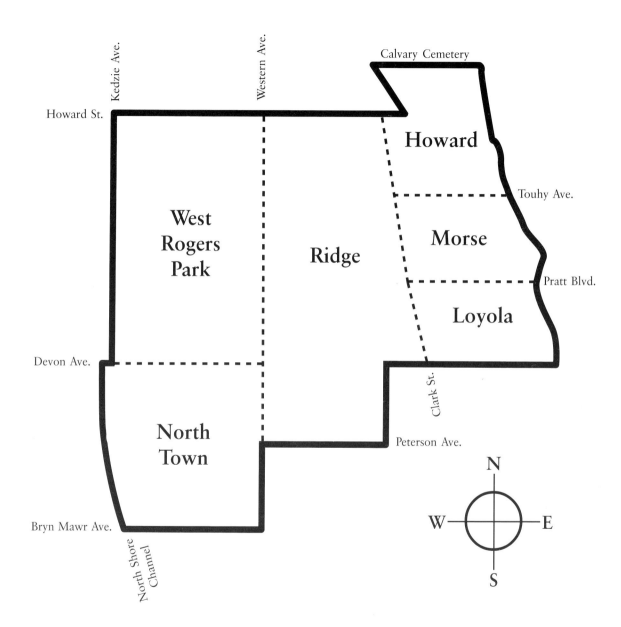

Looking Back: A Personal Retrospective of Rogers Park, West Rogers Park and the World
By Ira Berkow

A quest for the nation's greatest blintz ended at the door of Sam Ashkenaz's steamy, clattery, pungent kitchen on Morse Avenue in the heart of Rogers Park.

It happened this way. One morning in 1975, Barbara Walters in her *Not For Women Only* network television show, planned a week of ethnic food specials. Staff researchers were assigned to locate the most ambrosial restaurants of five nationalities in the country. For Jewish-style cooking, Ashkenaz Restaurant and Delicatessen was chosen.

The beloved and no-nonsense proprietor, the balding, sixty-one-year-old Sam Ashkenaz himself, with glasses gleaming under the TV lights, and natty in tied and clean white apron, wowed them by whipping up his stupendous, succulent and yes, beautiful "Ashkenaz Cheese Blintz Treat," topped, naturally, with fresh blueberries -- I emphasize fresh since the congealed frozen variety generally found elsewhere wouldn't have lasted five minutes with

Sam or his picky patrons. For good measure, Sam added a decent dollop of sour cream to the inimitable blintz.

I had heard about the show in advance, so tuned in at my apartment in Manhattan -- I had left Chicago a decade earlier to find my way in the thickets of journalism, ending up in New York City.

Watching Sam fry up those blintzes brought back memories of my having grown up on Chicago's North Side. I could nearly *smell* the food -- the sniff of blintzes gave way to the corned beef whose aroma soaked into the restaurant's woodwork and the homemade gefilte fish with a horseradish that produced the breath of a dragon. Surely there is nothing as evocative as smell to give the spur to memory, and so...

In the summer of 1953, at age thirteen, I moved with my family from the West Side after graduating Bryant Grammar School to the neighborhood we called West Rogers Park at

Granville and Mozart (pronounced in Chicago as though the composer spelled his name with an "s"). I was not unfamiliar with the North Side. I had often visited my first cousin, now federal magistrate, Ian Levin, at his home on Estes Avenue, near Loyola Park. It was at Loyola that the Indians, a team in the relatively new Little League that played its games at Thillens Stadium on Devon Avenue, practiced. I tried out and made the team. Thillens Stadium is a scaled-down version of a big-league ballpark, with night-lights, electric scoreboard and seats for around 5,000 spectators. It was exciting. I became the only player at Thillens from the West Side.

On Wednesday evenings, the games were televised on WGN with Jack Brickhouse, the Cubs' broadcaster, announcing from the small raised press box. The first time my team played on television, my family stayed home to watch. I remember striking out and going back to the dugout, cursing under my breath. Little did I know the camera was following me. I also got a hit in the game. After making the long journey home, I expected my parents to be proud of my newfound celebrity. My mother greeted me at the door. "Where," she demanded, "did you learn that kind of language? On the North Side?"

I didn't, of course, since the streets of the West Side were education enough in that area. But I would learn a lot on the North Side especially after moving there, and much of it good.

In September of 1953, I began my freshman year of high school at Sullivan -- just a few short blocks from Ashkenaz, I would learn -- and now embarked on the strange, ambiguous and ambivalent process of growing up.

I discovered girls and entered a weird new world of uncertainties and strivings and passions. I remember a warm spring day when I was walking north on Greenview near Sullivan with my friend Ronnie Berz. Across the street, coming in the other direction, was a teenage girl about our age in a tight, white sweater and pink shorts. She was pretty and God had not been sparing in his generosity to other salient aspects of her. Ronnie and I looked, or gaped, and then Ronnie slapped the top of his right hand quick as a jackhammer five or six times into the flattened palm of his left. Nothing else about young love and lust needed to be said. It was as eloquent a statement on the subject as I've ever heard.

Sports remained significant to my interests -- to the virtual exclusion, unfortunately, of my studies. Years later, when I went back to Sullivan to get my transcripts to aid in research

Ashkenaz Restaurant and Delicatessen, 1967. Photograph by Ed Jarecki. (Courtesy of the Chicago Sun-Times.)

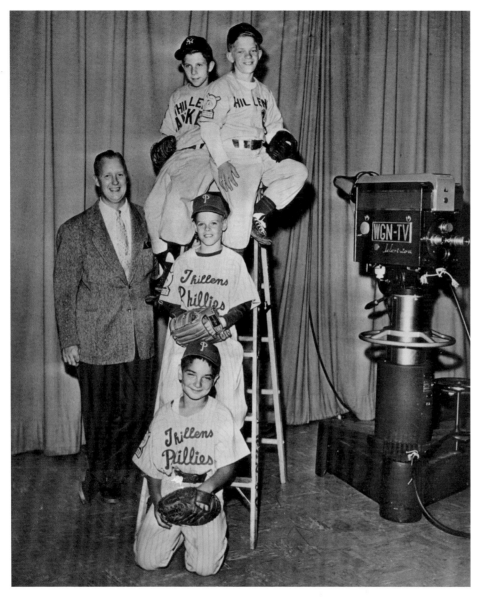

WGN broadcaster Jack Brickhouse with Thillens' Little League ballplayers, c. 1955.

for a book I was writing, the clerk made a copy of them and, walking toward me, happened to glance at them. "Oh," she said, rather sheepishly, as she saw I had spotted her, "I see you were very good in gym."

I did get an education at Sullivan, in spite of myself. There were some good teachers, none more important to me, however, than my basketball coach, Art Scher. He was a short, white-haired, reserved man with an enthusiasm for the game, but with perspective. He was an influence in my life. In my senior year, I was president of the Letterman's Club, with Coach Scher as the faculty advisor. As such, both he and I signed the certificate entitling a player to the "S," as chosen by the coaches. I was surprised to see that he was awarding a letter to a player, another senior, who had given him a hard time during the season and hadn't played much. I wasn't opposed to giving the player the letter, but I wondered why the coach had made that decision.

"Because," Coach Scher explained to me, "I don't want him to leave school with a bad taste in his mouth."

My dad, Harold Berkow, was a Democratic precinct captain in the 50th Ward, and in the Boss Daley years this meant the precinct captain was a kind of godfather in his particular domain. My dad got me an excellent-paying summer job on a city garbage truck -- I still have the original working card from 1956 with the title, "T.A. Laborer." (T.A. for Temporarily Assigned.) In the four summers I collected garbage, I came to intimately know virtually every alley and garbage can in the ward. It was a priceless kind of education, though I imagine, not everybody's cup of tea.

After adjusting to the smell at the back of the truck that nearly buckled my knees the first day, I eased into the job. In my first week I was assigned to a three-man crew (plus the driver) that included a black man, Donald Groves, a father of two daughters. Donald and I hit it off. We'd stop for a break and one of the guys would buy a round of soft drinks. Another break, and another guy would buy a round. And another. I thought this was terrific. I was sixteen years old, and guys were buying me stuff. At one point, though, Donald pulled me aside. He pointed out that each of the others had treated for drinks.

"I'm telling you this only because I like you, Ira, but you have to go into your pocket, too." It had never dawned on me. I was embarrassed. But Donald had saved me mortification by saying gently, "I'm telling you this only because I like you, Ira." I have never forgotten it, as well as that an important lesson in communication was taught to me by a garbage collector.

No one on the North Side, or anywhere else, has been as instrumental in my life as my parents. It was my father, however, who one day changed my life, though neither of us knew it at the time. I had torn ligaments in my ankle in a basketball game my senior year and was on crutches and home from school for several days. While I had been an avid reader in grade school, I had for the most part gotten out of the habit. One morning in our apartment at 6224 N. Mozart, my dad handed me a book, *30 Days to a More Powerful Vocabulary*. "You should read

something," he said, "and words are power." I put the book aside, of course, but it began to pique my curiosity. I opened it up. I was like Alice falling into the dark hole and winding up in Wonderland. I devoured the book.

I'd even go on a date and try to teach a girlfriend words from the book, like "loquacity" and "obsequious" and "pusillanimous."

"You," she said, "should see a doctor."

I had no idea, but this was the first step toward immersing myself in a lifetime of words.

There's more about Rogers Park and West Rogers Park that remains an elemental part of me, where alone or with friends I would spend hours and days from Green Briar Park to Indian Boundary (and the cozy zoo with my favorite, the grandly snouted cautimundi) to the outdoor basketball court at St. Jerome's to the Granada Theater to Red Hot Ranch on Devon Avenue to Welcome Inn (and its nonpareil thin-crusted pizza) on Western Avenue to the jouncy California Avenue bus to the Morse and Farwell Avenue Beaches.

I would go away to college, Miami University in Oxford, Ohio, and return to the Northwestern University Medill Graduate School of Journalism. I went into the Army (the six-month program), was a reporter starting in 1965 for the *Minneapolis Tribune*, became a sports columnist and general columnist for Newspaper Enterprise Association in New York, a Scripps-Howard feature syndicate, and joined the *New York Times* in 1981, where I'm a sports columnist and senior writer. I've been married and divorced and married again. I've met heads of state and jewel thieves. I've traveled.

And while it has been nearly four decades since I've lived in Chicago, I've never gotten Chicago and the North Side out of my blood. I've never gotten Ashkenaz out of my taste buds. Besides being one of the great eateries of Western Civilization, Ashkenaz was a gathering place for the kids after school and particularly on Friday nights, following a movie usually at the Granada. Both places swarmed with teenagers worrying about their place in the universe as well as their complexions.

Alas, Ashkenaz is gone now, torn down, not a brick or pickled herring left. Its departure from this earth several years ago, beginning I guess, because of a changing neighborhood, is still deeply lamented. It ought to have been named a national landmark and preserved, like the log cabin Lincoln was born in, for example. Instead, a parking lot -- a parking lot! -- exists where Ashkenaz once proudly and aromatically stood.

I will never forget the motto printed on the check you were handed at Ashkenaz. It read: "Better than this there isn't!"

Growing up is invariably mixed with pain and pleasure. But in my fondest memories of my life and times in Rogers Park and West Rogers Park, I find that the motto on the check at Ashkenaz said it better than I ever could.

Ira Berkow is a Pulitzer Prize-winning sports columnist for the New York Times, and the author of several books including Maxwell Street, To The Hoop, *and* How To Talk Jewish.

Remembrances of Rogers Park in the 1940s
by Hugh Downs

My wife and I moved into a one-bedroom, third floor apartment at 1644 W. Farwell in February 1944, that rented for $35 a month. We lived there for six years and our son and daughter were born there. We got to know the neighborhood pretty well and still enjoy the memories of living there until 1951 when we moved to Wilmette for a few years before going to New York City.

I remember the Farwell Drugstore on the northeast corner of Farwell and Clark, and Hy Katz, the owner and druggist. Since I would often take the Clark Street streetcar to go downtown, I used to stop in the drugstore for my morning cup of coffee. Hy also served as our family's pharmacist. My other choice for transportation downtown to the Merchandise Mart, and my announcing job at NBC's Central Division, was the elevated train that I would board at the Morse Avenue stop. Ashkenaz was a favorite place, and we used to visit the Farwell and Morse beaches on a regular basis in the summer.

I have a picture of me lying on the beach with my two-year-old daughter sitting on my stomach in a contemplative mood.

One of my strongest memories was early one evening, when I was walking home from the Morse 'El', and was set upon by what I can only conclude was a rabid squirrel. Luckily, I had my briefcase with me, because the squirrel, with distorted and foam-flecked lips and red eyes, charged me and I hit it with the briefcase. The squirrel attacked again, I hit it again, and it ran away. I'm lucky that it didn't bite me or I think that I could have had a serious medical problem.

I also remember the snowstorms we had while I was living in Rogers Park. One winter, I was pulling my young son on Farwell on a sled that had bucket-like seats. My head was bowed against the heavy west wind and the snowdrifts were piling up around us. All of a sudden, the sled pulled harder and when I looked back, I saw the sled was upside down and found that my son

had fallen off into a snowdrift. He wasn't very happy with me, but he was unhurt.

There were a couple of empty lots on the 1600 block of Farwell, one to the west of our building and one to the north, across the alley toward Morse Avenue. In 1945, I built a telescope in the basement of our building and spent quite a bit of time grinding and polishing the mirror on a pedestal and pitch-lap. It took about a year to complete it, and when it was finished I set it up in that empty lot and aimed it at the moon. A cop came over and wanted to know what I was doing. He said that the long barrel of the telescope looked like a weapon. I explained to him what I was doing and invited him to look at the moon through it because I was afraid that he thought I was a peeping tom. He enjoyed the view and went away impressed.

One of our neighbors on Pratt, and my colleague at the NBC Central Division, was Dave Garroway. I went to New York in 1954 to do the *Home Show*, and Dave had already moved to

New York in 1952 to become the star of the *To-day Show*. While he was in Chicago, Dave was on the *1160 Club*, and I used to go over to visit him at his apartment on Pratt. One time I went over to watch him chrome plating the front bumper of a Rolls Royce that he had rescued from a junkyard. In fact, he restored the entire car, including the paint.

When we lived in the neighborhood, our family attended St. Paul's By-the-Lake Episcopal Church located at Estes and Ashland. Once, my son came home from Sunday school with a pocketful of quarters. We wondered where he had been able to get so much money. We learned that when they had passed around the collection plate, he thought that it was something he could take with him. We had to go back to the church with him so that he could return the money.

As I look back on our years in Rogers Park, I can still remember the beautiful Dutch Elms that lined the streets, the chance to sled down the hills on Ridge Boulevard, and going to the Adelphi, the 400, and the Granada Theaters. We've lived a lot of places since, but some of our fondest memories are of Rogers Park.

Hugh Downs, is an Emmy award-winning broadcaster for NBC and ABC Television. He served as announcer for Caesar's Hour *and the* Tonight Show, *and was also anchor for the* Today Show *and* 20/20. *He currently lives outside of Phoenix, Arizona, and helped to establish The Hugh Downs School of Human Communication at Arizona State University.*

Winners of Boy Scout contest at the Granada Theater, 1946. Photograph by Henry Green. (Courtesy of the Chicago Historical Society, ICHi 25614.)

"Rose-Colored" Memories of West Rogers Park
by Steve Friedman

When I look back on growing up in West Rogers Park in the mid-fifties and early-sixties, the "rose" in "rose-colored glasses" just gets rosier. As I've traveled from Chicago to Los Angeles and, since 1979, to New York, I feel that the days of my childhood were probably even better than I remember. But, who cares, because as Dean Martin once sang, *Memories Are Made of This*.

Any look backward has to begin with the food. Most of it would be called "junk food," but to us it was "Chicago gourmet." I can still smell the Vienna hot dogs with mustard, relish and onions and grease-laden fries at Lerner's or the Hot Dog Ranch, and then later at places like Fluky's. Then, when it was time for pizza, there was always Oddo's or Il Forno's. The burgers came from one of the first McDonald's on Kedzie, the corned beef from Friedman's Delicatessen (no relation) on Western Avenue, and the ribs from across the street at Sally's. There were, what we called, full-service spots like Randl's and the Gold Coin, but we never had a lot of time to sit and eat -- we were always on the move.

All roads led to three basic places: Clinton School, Green Briar Park, and the alley behind our two-flat at 6133 N. Campbell. God Bless Mayor Richard J. Daley for putting lights in the alley so that we could play night baseball, football and basketball games. I'm sure that we were the only city of our size with streetlights in the alleys.

One of the best things about the '50s in Chicago's neighborhoods was the way that people took care of each other. If your mom or dad wasn't around, there was always an aunt, uncle or family friend to help out and, in my case, to bail me out of what we called "trouble." Back then it was stuff like talking back to teachers or making sure you were well-informed by stealing a *Chicago Sun-Times* from Walsh's Drug Store. Yes, it was a simpler time.

Many of us lived with or next door to our grandparents. Now, kids don't even live in the same time zone with their grandparents. With all the divorces in modern day America, they see mom or dad on weekends. That's not the way we grew up. If there is one change for the worst in this computer-driven world, it is the missing sense of community -- a sense of living somewhere and belonging to a neighborhood.

There also were our after-school and summer pleasures. When I grew up, it was spring and summer in the bleachers at Wrigley Field or the backstretch at Arlington Park. It cost seventy-five cents for a ticket to see the Cubs in the late '50s and early '60s, but there were no crowds. We watched one of the greatest hitting shortstops and one of the worst baseball teams in history. Outside of the great Ernie Banks, we learned how NOT to play America's great game. My buddies and I were the original "Bleacher Bums." We'd arrive early and terrorize visiting ballplayers and by June we would turn our wrath on the last place Cubs. As my friend, Barry Gifford, wrote in his excellent book, *The Neighborhood of Baseball*, we were in the first row in right centerfield and we ruled the area. We were regulars at Wrigley Field, and that included telling Cincinnati Reds outfielder Frank Robinson to show us his gun (he had been arrested earlier that year for carrying an unlicensed weapon) or throwing our version of mink-lined shoes on the field to the recently divorced Willie Mays. We had more fun before the game than we did during the game. There were also our favorite regulars including Warren Spahn of the Milwaukee Braves, Bob Purkey of the Reds and any Los Angeles Dodger. We hated the owners of the Dodgers for leaving New York because the night games started so late we could never listen to them on the radio.

One of our favorite Cub "victims" was a journeyman outfielder named Don Landrum. He wasn't very good -- a left-handed slap-hitter -- while we all preferred the home run hitters. "Donny", as we called him, made one of the biggest mistakes one could make at Wrigley Field -- he ignored us. Then, on a rainy day in June, he broke his silence. He told us to not only lay off him, but everyone else. He said that every guy out there had been a star in high school and all they were trying to do was just to make a living. Our response was to give him a standing ovation, an acknowledgment that he had talked to us even if it was a scolding. The next day Donny came out to right field with a peace offering that included balls and bats, and for me, one of his old baseball gloves. From then until the next year when he was traded, Donny was our man -- the "king of batting practice." Now, nearly forty years later, I have been able to reestablish contact with Donny. He has been ill, but he knows

that he has an open invitation for a free visit to New York so that I can show him a bat I saved with his autograph on it. As all Chicagoans can attest -- we remember our friends.

As for the racetrack, there were two reasons to go there -- when you had enough money and when you didn't. If you were broke, you waited until after the Seventh Race at Sportsmen's Park, parked by the railroad tracks, and hiked over the mud and the rails and got in free. That just gave you more money to bet on the races. When money was available, you went to the Clubhouse at Arlington Park. There are many racetrack stories from those years, but the most serious one happened in the summer of 1962 when my pal "Wild Bill" lost so much money and was in such debt that his parents called the cops and the Racing Board to put an end to his underage betting. Track rules said that no one under eighteen could get in without an adult. For a day or two, we were worried that our summer at Arlington would be ruined because cops had been stationed at the admittance gates. We decided to beat this by finding racetrack bums and making them our favorite "uncles." At first, it was tough to find these new "relatives," but when we offered each guy $10 to get us in, you would be surprised how many uncles we were able to find.

Green Briar Park was the center of our sixteen-inch softball universe. Catch the ball off the trees and it was an out. Jeff Ades made a career out of being the best "tree-catcher" at the park. During our first summer back from college in 1965 we met for a reunion game. One of the guys, "Be-Bop", was driving a cab to help

pay college bills. He stopped by, said that he couldn't play because he had to work, but was soon convinced to join the game. Unfortunately, Be-Bop forgot to turn his meter off. The game cost him $50, but it was well worth it because he had three hits and his team won.

There are many more memories: the field hockey games (there were no ice rinks); the fastball, rubber ball pitching games at Clinton; the Nehi Orange drinks after the games; the no-helmet, no-pads football games where blood and guts were the result; and the "plunge" games in the snow when three guys got together and bashed each other trying to pretend to be Jim Brown or Rick Casares.

As I look back on our years in West Rogers Park, I realize that what we learned on the streets and at home gave us a strong foundation for later lives. While it is a long way from Campbell Avenue to New York's Media Center, I learned three lessons that guide me now: 1) An honest day's work for an honest day's pay, whether delivering pizzas or producing the NBC Nightly News; 2) What's important are family and friends; and 3) Be honest, because you will have to tell the truth someday. So, to my parents and all the people who were there, thanks for the foundation of life, and of course, thanks for the memories.

Steve Friedman is senior executive producer of CBS' The Early Show, and was previously the producer of NBC's Today Show and Nightly News.

Rogers Park and West Ridge: Past and Present
by U.S. Representative Jan Schakowsky

I am not a historian or a demographer, but I know the community areas of Rogers Park and West Ridge. For over half a century, I have lived within a three-mile circle, the psychological, if not physical center of which, is commonly referred to as West Rogers Park. It represents both my past and my present. But while riding my bike no-handed around my neighborhood, I never dreamed that it would be "my district" and I would be its representative in the United States Congress.

I was born Janice Lynn Danoff in 1944 and lived with my mother, father and sister in a second floor apartment at 6147 N. Mozart until I was seven years old. I can clearly envision every room in that apartment though I haven't been in it for fifty years. My father planted a "Victory Garden" in the field behind our house where I loved searching with my dad for the little strawberries. My mother would wheel me in a stroller to Devon Avenue where she would exchange ration coupons for meat and chicken at the butcher

shop. We lived directly across the street from Clinton School, so close that we could hear the school bell. My sister Debby, ten years my senior, rang the bell, and I was proud each time I heard it. When I finally was old enough to go to school, I had the same kindergarten teacher that Debby had, and we cheerfully complained about mean Ms. Aulfrey. My aunt and cousins lived in the next building, and everyone on the block knew each other. Illinois State Senator Art Berman was a Mozart Street boy.

In 1951, we moved into a cozy three-bedroom house at 2542 W. Jarvis and I enrolled in Rogers School. Only about half the block was built up at that time, but since West Rogers Park was the new place to live, homes sprouted up quickly. My world consisted of grammar school, Temple Menorah for Hebrew school and Sunday school, my friends, and our weekly Sunday visit to my maternal grandparents in Humboldt Park. My mother, a devoted teacher, returned to work when we moved and would regularly substitute

at Rogers School, once in a while in my classroom to my embarrassment and delight.

In the spring, the lawns would be white with cottonwood seeds. I would climb the big trees and wish for a horse or a dog. One day a patrol boy who lived in one of the Quonset huts next to Rogers School, and who always teased me (my mother said it was because he liked me), gave me a dog -- Snippy. My dad built a pony-sized wooden horse that I would "pretend ride" in the basement for hours on end. My friend David Gerber and I would play in the woods where the Howard-Western shopping center now stands and throw Osage oranges into the street, until the day we hit a car and the driver told our parents. We would bowl at the Howard Bowl and go to the Howard or Nortown theaters on Saturday afternoons. Life was sweet.

The #151 bus took me to Sullivan High School where I played in the band and sang in the girls' choir. I tried out for cheerleader and settled for pom-pom girl. I met Neal Samors, the co-author of this book, and "went steady" with Eddie Brown. I ran for class secretary and lost to Eddie Mogul, and then I ran for Vice President and won. I ate at Ashkenaz and sometimes on Friday nights hung out at the Granada Theatre. I burned my skin at Morse beach in the summer.

As a newlywed in 1965, I lived at Fargo and Oakley on the second floor, where we paid $90 a month rent. It was a quiet street, right across from St. Scholastica's field. Our son, Ian, was born there. I would push the buggy over to grandma and grandpa's house every day. When I became pregnant with Mary, we moved to the northwest suburbs for a few years, the only time in my life that I've lived out of the immediate area.

My mother, Tillie Danoff, lived on Jarvis until she died, and my dad, Irwin, or Irv, stayed on alone in the house for another four years. Then he came to live with me in Evanston, less than two miles from his old house. Each day he would go to the Belden Deli at Howard and Western for brunch. When he died in 1997, the Belden closed and somehow it felt fitting.

"Home" means something very different to everyone. For me, it is the streets and homes, schools and shops, the synagogues and churches, the parks and beaches that make up Rogers Park, West Rogers Park and now Evanston, where I have lived (not far from the Howard Street border) for nearly thirty years. As a girl I shopped on Devon at Debs and Heirs and Carol Korr. Now I go to a vibrant Devon Avenue for Indian food or to meet friends from the Pakistani, Bangladesh, or Indian communities. Robert Hall, the clothing store for men, has been renovated and is now the Croatian Cultural Center, and while there is

still an active Jewish presence on Devon, many of the residents now come from the former Soviet Union. My old blocks and homes look loved, and some of my Jarvis Avenue neighbors are still there.

As a child, my world was predominantly Jewish and my schools were nearly empty on Jewish holidays. Today Rogers Park and West Ridge are two of the most diverse communities in the country. They are gateways to the United States for people from around the globe. More than forty languages are spoken at each of the high schools. Families choose to live in Rogers Park and West Ridge for the very same reasons that my parents bought our house there -- good schools, good neighbors, good transportation, safe streets, nice homes and apartments, and wonderful parks and beaches.

The political and civic leaders of my youth have given way to a new generation of leaders who have been dedicated stewards of the community, investing in its infrastructure and its people. Children growing up in Rogers Park and West Ridge today are building their own memories in neighborhoods that have faced the challenges of the years and have emerged in a characteristically unpretentious way as models for successful twenty-first century communities.

U.S. Congresswoman Jan Schakowsky (D-IL) was first elected to Congress in 1998 and represents Illinois' 9th Congressional District. She is in her second term. She was previously a State Representative for eight years from Illinois' 18th District.

Top: Ground breaking ceremony for new addition at Rogers School, c.1950. (Courtesy of the Chicago Park District.)

Bottom: Rogers School Park playground, 1958. (Courtesy of the Chicago Park District.)

The Loyola Neighborhood

Boundaries:
Devon Avenue to Pratt Boulevard (S-N)
Lake Michigan to Clark Street (E-W)

In 1900, the Loyola neighborhood was little more than a sandy, bush- and tree-filled section of the recently annexed Chicago neighborhood of Rogers Park. The Chicago, Milwaukee & St. Paul Railroad had built tracks that stretched from Wilson Avenue through Rogers Park, Evanston and Wilmette, but there was limited service on the line. The tracks would later become the Chicago Transit Authority's elevated line from Chicago to Wilmette.

The neighborhood was the focal point for the new St. Ignatius Parish. The Jesuits purchased the property on March 9, 1906, for $161,254 from the Chicago, Milwaukee & St. Paul. They used the land to build the original St. Ignatius Church, Loyola University and Loyola Academy. St. Ignatius Parish continued to grow

in the 1910s and most of the membership was second- and third-generation Irish whose fathers and grandfathers had come from Ireland to build the Illinois and Michigan Canal in the 1830s. They had educated their children at St. Ignatius on the West Side of Chicago, and their children were the dominant group in the new parish in the Loyola neighborhood.

A new St. Ignatius Church was built in 1917 at Loyola and Glenwood Avenues, and the church, school and convent would become the center of life for parish families throughout the twentieth century. To many Irish Catholic residents of the neighborhood, the section around St. Ignatius would be known as "The Patch." Bill Nellis refers to the church and Loyola Academy as "two closely related citadels of my youth in Rogers Park."

In 1926, the site of the original St. Ignatius Church became the location of the Granada Theatre, a movie palace that would remain a neighborhood institution for the next

sixty years. In the early years, theatergoers could also see stage shows and participate in sing-alongs. By the 1940s, the Granada had become the most popular movie house on Chicago's Far North Side. Other movie theaters in the neighborhood included the Regent (later The 400; currently the Village North) on Sheridan Road, and the Ridge on Devon, east of Clark (originally the Ellantee).

During the 1920s, the Loyola neighborhood experienced a major building boom as dozens of brick three- and four-story apartment buildings were constructed, along with homes, apartment-hotels, grocery stores, pharmacies, restaurants and businesses of all varieties. It was the beginning of significant population growth for the neighborhood as thousands of new residents moved in. Herschel Oliff lived in the Loyola neighborhood at 6450 N. Wayne Avenue from 1921 to 1928 and then at 1309 W. Arthur Avenue from 1928 to 1940. "I started kindergarten at the Kilmer portables on Loyola Avenue,

just west of the elevated tracks. It was a mixed neighborhood of Jews and Catholics, as well as other Christian faiths."

Lilian Minkus moved to 1248 W. Albion in the 1920s. "My father was one of the founders of Congregation B'nai Zion that formed in 1919. The congregants first used the Episcopal Church on Lunt as a place of worship until they eventually moved to Pratt and Greenview where the sanctuary was built in 1925. By the late 1940s, B'nai Zion had grown to more than 1,000 members and had to close its membership because it had grown so fast."

Catholics and Jews interacted regularly as neighbors, but their children attended different grammar schools, usually after completing kindergarten at Kilmer Elementary School. The children of Catholic families often went to St. Ignatius Elementary School for first through eighth grades and then on to such high schools as Loyola Academy, for boys and St. Scholastica, for girls, while the Jewish kids continued at Kilmer and then went to Sullivan High School.

Loyola University and Mundelein College, built in 1930 next to the university, are also institutions that remain vital parts of the Loyola neighborhood today.

Among the Irish Catholic residents who settled in the Loyola neighborhood in the early years of the twentieth century were the Hartigans, who had come to Rogers Park around the time that St. Ignatius parish was being established in the 1910s. Coletta Hogan Hartigan came to the neighborhood from the west side, went to Holy Child High School on Sheridan Road and helped to found the famous Loyola Community Theater and the Green Room Players. David Hartigan attended Northwestern University and Loyola University Law School, and served as the 49th Ward Alderman in the 1940s and 1950s until he was elected Chicago's City Treasurer in 1955, and re-elected in 1959. He would be instrumental in saving the beaches in the Loyola neighborhood from high-rise development and today, the beach and park at Albion are named in his honor.

Frank 'Tweet' Hogan was a star athlete

Loyola University Commencement, 1932. (Courtesy of Loyola University Archives.)

Clark Street looking north from Devon, 1930. (Courtesy of the CTA.)

at Loyola Academy and Loyola University. He would become a famous bandleader, open the Drake Hotel when he was 19 years old, perform with his band on network radio shows, and start the "Chicago School of Comedians" that included Shelly Berman, George Gobel, and Bob Newhart. Frank's wife, Monica, one of the Skelly sisters, played the Palace.

Neil Hartigan, who was at various times 49th Ward Committeeman, Illinois Attorney General and Lieutenant Governor, continues to live in the Loyola neighborhood. He remembers the neighborhood and the St. Ignatius Parish as a place where "people knew and cared about each other. Rogers Park was like a village where you didn't have one set of parents, you had fifty sets of parents and the idea that there was any difference because of religion or race didn't seem to occur to anybody."

The Holy Child nuns taught the students at St. Ignatius School. Bill Nellis recalls that kids "never wandered out of the neighborhood until their teenage years." For him and his friends, "the neighborhood boundaries were Devon and Pratt, and Ashland and the Lake. Wagtayles Restaurant on Loyola was a big hangout on Sunday mornings. And, on special occasions, we would go there for waffles." Neil Hartigan recalls, "I got up in the morning and walked out the door, crossed Glenwood and was at school. It was fun. There were thirty kids in a class, and, academically, it was a very good school, although I remember that some of the nuns were tough as nails."

An important tradition in the Loyola neighborhood in the late 1940s was the weekly softball game between the Catholic and Jewish teams, usually made up of a combination of teenagers and WWII veterans. They would meet on Sunday mornings at the gravel playground at the south end of Sullivan High School on Albion. "I remember Joe Fisher who was a pitcher for the Jewish team," said Bill Nellis. "I don't think he ever cracked a smile, but he was a very good player."

Although the Catholics and the Jews were well represented at those games, there were other sites of sports-related interactions between boys from the two religious groups in the neighborhood. According to Bob Dauber, kids from several religious persuasions would meet at the empty lot at Schreiber and Ashland for an annual football game in the 1950s. "That was an interesting area. East of Bosworth was a good mix of Jews and Protestants, while west of Bosworth to Clark Street was Catholics. We used to have an annual touch football game around Labor Day every year. It was kind of like the Jews against the Catholics."

The public schools in the neighborhood included Kilmer Elementary School, built in 1928, and Sullivan High School, which opened first as a junior high school in 1926 and then became a senior high school in 1930.

Judy Schwade Rozner has memories of Kilmer. "On my first or second day in kindergarten, I came home at recess because I thought that school was over. When I came in the house my mother asked me what I was doing there. I said, 'They let us out,' and she said, 'My dear, that was recess and you have to go back.' I quickly learned the ropes and I loved going to Kilmer

Mundelein College social room, 1938.
(Courtesy of the Mundelein College, Women and Leadership Archives.)

Loyola Ramblers versus Iowa Hawkeyes, 1962.
(Courtesy of the Loyola University Archives.)

for those nine years." Her sister, Janet Schwade Seichelman, agreed with her assessment, noting that, "the teachers were wonderful, from Ms. Mallen in first grade to Mrs. Sampson in fifth grade, to Mrs. Glass, the school librarian."

Dorothy Katz Berez moved to the Loyola neighborhood in seventh grade. "I remember that the kids were very friendly to me even though I was new in the neighborhood. It's really hard to start at a new school when you are twelve or thirteen years old, but the kids were great and we used to hang out together in the Kilmer playground. As I recall, the high school kids wouldn't let us hang around across North Shore Avenue at Sullivan High School."

Prior to 1926, kids from Rogers Park and West Rogers Park went to Senn High School on Glenwood near Ridge, and even after Sullivan was opened, many students from West Rogers Park opted to attend Senn. In 1959, when Mather High School was built at California and Peterson, many West Rogers Park teens went there.

In the 1940s, Cookie Brandt remembers that the girls at Sullivan "wore grays, lavenders and pinks. We played music at lunchtime in the Assembly Hall, danced on the stage, practiced putting on lipstick, and visited with friends. There were lots of dances. The clubs would rent huge ballrooms in downtown hotels, and we would go downtown on the 'El' for a date." Social clubs played a key role in high school life from the 1940s through the 1960s. Shelly Lang Berger remembers that "clubs were really, really important when we went to Sullivan in the late '50s. It was a means of acceptance. If you were either a Star or a Keg it was a big deal, and when you were selected to be in a club it was very exciting."

John Grigsby played basketball in the '50s when he attended Sullivan, but he remembers that Sam Fralick, the football coach, was persistent in trying to get him to also join the football team. "He was always yelling at me to join the football team, but I just didn't want to play. I enjoyed basketball and didn't need another sport. I also remember that we would have dances with clubs from other schools and we raised a lot of money for charities." For Betty Toben Warden, Sullivan was a wonderful college prep high school. "I mean, in the 1950s, we never really considered whether or not to go to college after high school. It was only a matter of which one we should attend. We had those wonderful Friday night dances, and I remember that Judy Schwade's mother and my mom used to teach dancing to the kids. My favorite teacher at Sullivan was my English teacher, Mrs. Prindes, because she really expanded our vocabularies and challenged us to excel."

Many teens attending Sullivan had perceptions about the differences between those from East Rogers Park and West Rogers Park. According to Bob Dauber, "we had a very heavy Jewish population at Sullivan. It was my observation that if an East Rogers Park Jewish kid would flunk a course, his father would swat him for his failure. If a West Rogers Park Jewish kid flunked a course, his father would buy him a Corvette. The kids from West Rogers Park seemed to look down at us, but I don't think that had any impact on our self-perception. It was very apparent to me that there were eco-

The Granada Theatre, 1964. (Courtesy of the CTA.)

Neil Hartigan at 49th Ward Office, c.1975.

nomic differences between East and West Rogers Park, and they were exhibited in the way we dressed and where we shopped."

Life in the Loyola neighborhood was much more than just attendance at educational institutions. In addition to Catholics and Protestants who attended churches in the area, many Jewish residents belonged to any one of the several synagogues in the neighborhood, including Congregation Beth Sholom, on Pratt near Sheridan, and Congregation Kesser Maariv, on Greenview near Devon. The best-known congregation, and the one with the largest membership, was Congregation B'nai Zion, the Conservative synagogue on Pratt at Greenview.

As for shopping, there were places such as Stells on Loyola, Russ Roeper's IGA on Devon, Fannie Mae Candy on Sheridan, Fleig's Bakery and Arfa's Bakery on Devon, Abe's Delicatessen on Sheridan, Buy-Low at Pratt and Ashland, Kroger on Sheridan, and R&N Food Mart on Devon.

There were the beaches at Loyola, Albion (later Hartigan Beach and Park), North Shore and Columbia. Eileen Deegan remembers going to Albion Beach in the 1950s. "The beach was a hang-out where the students from Loyola and Mundelein would gather. And, near Albion Beach, at Sheridan Road, there was the Pink Squirrel Lounge, and just south of the 'El' tracks, was Bob and Ed's where they would serve free sandwiches and show movies on Sundays."

Norman Mark recalls, "I was into running in the '70s and would often use the Loyola University track. I also remember walking one block from our apartment on Columbia to the beach. There were all of those 'secret' beaches between Loyola and Pratt as well as various places to play volleyball and hang out."

In the latter part of the twentieth century, changes began to occur in the Loyola neighborhood as new ethnic and racial groups moved in. A major concern was the increasing cost of housing that was slowly forcing individuals and families to explore other options. However, many long-time residents have remained in the neighborhood. Neil Hartigan, whose family has lived within a few blocks of St. Ignatius Church for almost ninety years, still owns a home on Albion and believes in the future of the neighborhood and in its stability. He and many other residents remain committed to maintaining the integrity of the community, keeping the housing costs under control, and assuring that the generations to come will seek to build their lives in a neighborhood that has a mix of rental apartments, condominiums and homes, and a diversity of people from many cultures, races and religions.

As Harold Ramis notes, "I loved living in Rogers Park because it was comfortable and safe. We knew every inch of our neighborhood and I still have very vivid memories of it. I drive through it and show my kids where I lived on Glenwood and Arthur, and all of the other places of interest during my youth in the Loyola neighborhood."

AIDS quilt on display at Loyola University, 1993. Photograph by Phil Moloitis.

Pratt and Southport (later Glenwood) looking east, c.1915. (Courtesy of the CTA.)

Mrs. Frank McLaughlin, interviewed in November 1927

In the first days of our life up here, the land from Albion to Farwell was prairie. There was a sand ridge running in the middle of the 1100 block from Devon to Touhy Avenue. There were so many big oaks from Sheridan Road to about a block east that you couldn't see the lake from Sheridan Road. East of the woods was the wide beach. The oaks died with the draining and sewerage. It's a shame, for they were so lovely. We have managed to keep one old one in our yard, but the largest ones died off.

John Dillon, interviewed in October 1927

I came to the Loyola district in 1907. The place where the college stands now used to be used as a picnic ground a long time ago. I recall having to get off the 'El' at Wilson Avenue. We used to meet our friends who were coming out from the city at the Wilson Avenue stop and drive them out to Rogers Park. My partner can tell you about coming home at two o'clock in the morning and waiting for the milk wagon to hop a ride on up to Rogers Park.

There used to be a real estate office, but it was only an old shack, at the elevated and Sheridan Road where Henderson's Real Estate office is now. Sheridan Road was pretty muddy just there, and when you stepped off the doorsill onto the plank laid down in front of the door, you splashed yourself with mud. Instead of these apartments, there used to be frame houses when I came here first. Someone built a two-story building at the corner of Pratt and Sheridan that was used for apartments. People said the man was crazy, but the building still stands and the people came to realize that they could not afford to live in single dwellings when taxes were so high. Rogers Park was like an outgrown village until the last two years when big flats, hotels and the Granada Theatre came in. Now it has a city atmosphere.

Policeman, Sheridan and Devon, interviewed in November 1927

Yes, sir, I've been on this beat for twenty years. I guess I ought to know something about this community. Before that, about thirty years ago I worked for the streetcar company. They were putting in the Devon line at that time. The only thing around here thirty years back was Jaeger's tavern at the corner of Devon and Sheridan Road. That's the same building you see now. There were two frame houses, or maybe only one was frame and the other brick. Anyway, Jacob Sickenger's stood where it is now at Greenview and there was a brick one on Sheridan Road north of the 'El.' The first people out here were the Irish, all right. They used to have a lot of gardens, regular truck farms, and then even later, people had their own little garden on the end of their lot. I have made only three arrests in the past year. I guess that's a good enough neighborhood for you.

Marshal Foch, Commander in Chief of Allied Armies in W.W.I, in front of Dumbach Hall, Loyola University, 1921. (Courtesy of Loyola University Archives.)

Sullivan High School swim class, c.1930.

Mundelein College students in front of Piper Hall, 1937. (Courtesy of Mundelein College, Women and Leadership Archives.)

Water Carnival at Mundelein College, 1938. (Courtesy of Mundelein College, Women and Leadership Archives.)

Granada Theatre, c.1930. (Courtesy of the CTA.)

John James, former Granada head usher

My interest in the Granada goes back to the years 1942 through early 1945. Mr. R. C. Macmullen -- Mr. "Mac" as we called him -- was the manager of the Granada for many years. Most folks remember him in his white summer tuxedo or his formal winter attire, changing in the evening into a tux. My job was Chief of Service, or head usher. I told a fib about my age and got the job when I was a little younger than fifteen years old, instead of the required age of sixteen. I remember the red velvet ropes and the brass rails controlled the "hold back" crowds because every one of the 3,447 seats was sold out for the wartime movie *Mrs. Minniver*. I had the additional assignment of preparing the payroll at the theater. I remember how difficult it was to calculate the overtime compensation for the four projectionists -- time and a half for work prior to 12:30 p.m., double time for work after 1:00 a.m. As head usher, I made $.03 an hour more than the rest of the ushers, which brought my hourly rate up to $.37 an hour. I was convinced that my acne problem was related to my weekly assignment of being alone while taking inventory of the Granada's candy supplies.

The projectionists were members of a tight "fathers and sons" union and they earned a staggering $113.84 a week. I remember that these gentlemen had one $18.75 war savings bond deducted from their paychecks each week, more money than many of our employees made for a week's work. Our stagehand was Harry Hirsch.

Harry's main job was to raise and lower the fire curtain prior to and after each performance. Harry and our engineer maintained the theater's heat and air conditioning and drew $78.00 a week. A full-time female employee was present in the elaborate ladies room that also served as a "check room." She performed additional cleaning duties and earned $18.00 a week. Unlike the older, more dignified cashiers who were isolated in the glass ticket booth with strange, shiny brass ticket dispensing machines and cash boxes, the candy girls, although still a little older than the average usher, were more approachable. They would at least talk to the ushers, but Mr. Mac did not approve and he let us know it.

The usher force consisted of some eighteen young men (boys) who attended Sullivan, Senn and Amundsen High Schools. As head usher, I made the schedules that had varied duties depending upon whether one was assigned to opening or closing. Closing at 12:30 a.m. was difficult for some who had early classes the next day. Then, there was that nightly mail pouch containing attendance numbers and correspondence that had to be taken by streetcar to the Uptown Theatre after closing. I maintained the inventory of paper cardboard wing collars, dickeys, studs, collar buttons, white gloves and usher uniforms. On the back door of the old usher supply room, near the elevator on the third floor, was a hand written list of all the ushers who went into military service in WWII, including those who had been killed in action. I maintained this crude list on the closet door until I entered the

Marine Corps in April 1945.

After a report that theater tickets were being sold at some north side high schools, Balaban and Katz replaced all usher ticket takers with full-time adult employees. The first full-time ticket taker was a retired British enlisted man who had served twenty years in a Scottish Highland regiment stationed in India. Our young ushers were impressed.

There are so many memories: the elaborate upstairs manager's office with its shower; the player grand piano on the first level balcony; the "Paris Carnival Scene" painting in the men's room; the backstage dressing rooms that Mr. Mac finally allowed the ushers to use; the organ; the New Year's Eve sing-alongs; and the sheer beauty of the marble, velvet, and brass surroundings.

Draftees waiting to board chartered streetcar, Devon and Broadway, 1944. Photograph by Henry Green. (Courtesy of the Chicago Historical Society, ICHi 32262.)

Students at War Finance Committee meeting, 1454 W. Devon, 1944. Photograph by Henry Green. (Courtesy of the Chicago Historical Society, ICHi 32265.)

Victory Campaign Honor Roll, 1454 W. Devon, 1944. Photograph by Henry Green. (Courtesy of the Chicago Historical Society, ICHi 32264.)

Pvt. Martin Guthmann, Rogers Park resident

On December 8, 1941, the day after Pearl Harbor, Pvt. Martin L. Guthmann, wrote to his parents, "I think we all should be happy that I am well and able to do my bit for our country. The odds are greatly in my favor of never even seeing battle, but I hope I do. My spirit is good and I know no one has had such an enjoyable life as mine. I am proud to carry our name forward on any duty our government wishes. So, please don't worry and before we know it this whole thing will also come to pass."

Herschel Oliff, interviewed in 1994

In World War II, everybody went into the Army. It wasn't like Vietnam, you know, with protests -- you just went. After all, especially if you were Jewish, you were fighting Hitler and anti-Semitism. But, even non-Jews felt it was their duty to protect the country. This protesting was something that we were not used to in our generation and that is probably why there are such big differences of opinion. I think that in my generation we were more conservative in our thinking.

Jacqueline McNicol, interviewed in 1994

I graduated from Sullivan High School on January 18, 1942. There were already empty seats at our graduation because several of our classmates had enlisted immediately after Pearl Harbor. They placed mortarboards on the chairs to recognize those who were graduating in absentia. Things were never the same in the neighborhood, and there were just too many who didn't come back from World War II. However, for many of the servicemen and servicewomen who did return from the War, they had great difficulty finding an apartment to rent. There was little empty space in the neighborhood to build GI housing, and all of the apartment buildings and houses were filled.

Ridge Theatre, c.1940. (Courtesy of the Theatre Historical Society of America.)

Bob Dauber, creative consultant

I lived at Devon and Greenview in the '50s. At the corner of Devon and Bosworth was Jack's. It was a combination of a school supply store, soda fountain and sandwich shop. At Greenview and Devon was the Katz-Menzies Drugstore and we used to get ice cream sandwiches there after lunch. Another place I remember was Arfa's Bakery on Devon between Newgard and Glenwood. There was Blitz Shoe Store and a number of grocery stores, including a National Tea store. On the north side of Devon, there was a gas station owned by Bill Medjes. An American Legion hall was built on what used to be an empty lot at Devon and Newgard where we played baseball.

The movie theater that was the closest was the Ridge Theatre. It was at Clark and Devon and you could go there for the whole day for about a dime. At one time it was called the Ellantee Theatre (it was originally part of the Lubiner and Tring theater chain). They would have two or three feature movies and a whole bunch of serials. I would get deposited there for an entire Saturday. I remember that the Ridge would sometimes hold raffles in the evenings and give away prizes like bicycles and dishes. I also recall an occasional encounter with rodents that had an affinity for the trash and a floor surface that hadn't been cleaned in a while and to which our shoes would invariably stick. One time, at the soda vending machine, there was a cockroach that dropped into a cup I was using to get pop. Despite those unsavory events, I still remember the Ridge with great fondness and think it was a sad day when it closed because the other theater that was near our house was the Granada and it cost $.25 to go there.

Neil Hartigan, attorney and politician

The Ridge was a major theater in our neighborhood. It was located on Devon east of Clark. I wasn't there the day this happened, but the Ridge used to show Westerns. As I understand it, on one occasion, as the cowboys on the screen yelled "Draw," a boy in the theater took his BB gun out and shot the screen. In any event, the Ridge was a great place to see Westerns and war movies, as well as the popular serials.

St. Patrick's Day celebration at St. Ignatius, c.1940.

Loyola Community Theater performance at St. Ignatius, c.1940.

Loyola Community Theater's Salute to Youth of 1952.

Bill Nellis, union fund secretary

One of the most important neighborhood events in the '40s was the annual teenage show that was done at the Loyola Community Theater. The theater, with a main floor and a balcony, held about 1,000 people and was located between St. Ignatius Church and the school. When I went to school at St. Ignatius, you were lucky if you got to participate in the show. It was a Broadway-style show and professional people put it together, although the kids in the show were high school age. It was big-time in terms of the music, and it was always a contemporary show. I remember the year we did it was the year that Alaska and Hawaii came in as states. So, we had special things out of "South Pacific," including skits, and it was really a great show.

Marilyn Woitel, businesswoman

What I do remember about living in the Loyola area was the life of the St. Ignatius Parish in the '50s. It was a place that was very welcoming and there were always a lot of things for kids to do. In particular, what I remember most is they used to do a talent show. The variety show starred teens from St. Ignatius and was put together each year by the Hogan family with help from parents of students at the high school. I also remember that the parish had a high school hangout room where you could go and get help with your homework. It was just a place to go after school to be with other kids, feel safe, and have a place where you could socialize. There was a staff of volunteers, and I think neighborhood residents greatly appreciated having a place for teenagers to go after school. I spent a lot of time there, and, in the evenings, when I had finished my homework, I would go there.

Neil Hartigan, attorney and politician

The Community Theater at St. Ignatius was something that my mother, Coletta, was very active in. They called themselves the "Green Room Players," which was part of the six or seven element program that was put on at the Loyola Community Theater. There were all sorts of national acts that performed in the 1,000-seat theater, as well as the very popular teen-age shows that involved hundreds of kids. And, if a boy or girl from St. Ignatius was involved in the show, then his or her parents were involved. They might serve as ticket takers, or ushers, or part of the stage crew, but there was total community involvement in the theater.

Sullivan High School ROTC, c.1950. Photograph by Henry Green. (Courtesy of the Chicago Historical Society, ICHi 25607.)

Jim Kirkpatrick, computer specialist

When I was at Sullivan, from 1951 to 1955, I took ROTC and I remember Sgt. Flanders and Sgt. Gunderson. There was a firing range in the basement that we would use during ROTC and, in those days, if you had a rifle, you could take it to school. In fact, you could carry your rifle in its case as you rode to school on your bicycle, and nobody complained about it. That shows you that times have really changed.

Joan Reiter Downing, educator and author

I first began teaching English at Sullivan in 1957. It was considered a very desirable place to teach, and Rogers Park was recognized as a very nice neighborhood. I think that what made Sullivan a special school was the neighborhood and the strong family orientation. The parents cared a great deal that their children would be well educated and would learn in high school and you could feel it in the classes. I really enjoyed teaching at Sullivan because the students were very responsive and the parents were very caring about what was going on and how well the kids were doing.

Irwin Kanefsky, business owner

I went to Sullivan in the late '50s and early '60s and was on the baseball team as a starting pitcher. During the three years that I played baseball, I had three different coaches. In my sophomore year, Alex Nemcoff was the coach and he had been an institution at Sullivan for many years. But, he took a sabbatical in 1960 and some guy came in from another school to be the coach. The guy had been a swimming coach and didn't know much about baseball. So, during my senior year, Sam Fralick, who had been football coach and whose expertise was in soccer, became the baseball coach. Sam was a nice guy, and I think that his claim to fame was that he would stand at the gym all day and shoot baskets from half court. I remember that during the baseball team's spring practice in 1961, we went over to Rogers Park, at Washtenaw, north of Touhy. We started practicing in March, and since it was cold outside we would begin our practice in the Sullivan gym and take ground balls off the wooden floor. That was like taking your life in your own hands because the ball would just fly at you. And then, once the snow melted, and even though it was only forty degrees outside and pretty nasty weather, we would go to Rogers for some outdoor practice. Well, senior year, our coach didn't want to get out of his car while we were practicing. He preferred to wait for Cal's Kitchen, a mobile food truck, to come to the field. Cal would show up since he knew that we were practicing, and Sam would get out of his car just long enough to get some sandwiches, and then sit in his car and eat. And, since

Sam was a football coach, instead of a baseball coach, he would often come to me for advice on strategies. He would come up to me and say, "Hey, lefty, what do we do in this situation?" And my response might be, "Coach, we've got to bunt here." So, Coach Fralick would tell me, "Okay, just get up there and bunt." I liked playing baseball, and we had a good team and a good time.

Bob Dauber, creative consultant

The night I graduated from Sullivan in 1957, Mr. Brown, the band teacher came up to me and said, "Dauber, I'm going to miss you. I've been teaching in the Chicago Public School system for twenty-three years. You are undoubtedly one of the most creative and talented musicians I've ever had in my bands and orchestras, and you are unquestionably the biggest screw-up I've ever met in my life!" My mother loves that story, but I did excel in music. And, the school counselor, Ms. Stanton, said to me in my separation interview, "Bud," and she called everyone Bud, "You know, Bud, I've got a good mind not to let you go to college." And I said, "Why is that?" And she said, "Well, with the mind that you've got and the way you don't use it, it would just be a waste of time and money." So, my response was, "Well, shouldn't that decision be mine, and not yours?" I did ultimately graduate college, much to her chagrin.

Boy Scouts at groundbreaking ceremony for new addition, Congregation B'nai Zion, 1950.

Congregation B'nai Zion Purim activities, c.1950.

Congregation B'nai Zion Hebrew class, c.1950.

Marshall Dermer, college educator

I was sent to B'nai Zion where I spent four years, completely unmotivated. Somehow, amazingly, I did learn how to read Hebrew. The only thing I remember is that I felt very sheltered during the High Holiday services. The deep resonant voices of men praying made me feel protected and I thought that was special.

David Schultz, attorney

I went to B'nai Zion in the '50s, although I personally did not have any affinity for religious experience and study. I was not a rebellious child, but I did my share of cutting Hebrew school classes. I felt that it was not a natural fit for me. My mother sang in the choir at B'nai Zion and the whole family was there often. It was kind of like getting in free because your mother was an usher at the ballgame and you could sneak in. On High Holidays, she was given tickets for the whole family. I was bar mitzvah because everybody else was and it seemed that every Saturday for a year I was going to friends' bar mitzvahs.

Betty Toben Warden, direct marketing consultant

The Purim festival was a big deal in the 1950s. We dressed up in costumes, and all of the girls wanted to be Queen Esther. It was held in Oliff Auditorium at B'nai Zion. There were games and things to buy and things to eat, like hamentashen, as well as prizes for best costumes and for winning the games. We had a wonderful time there and it was like a huge costume party. Everyone in the synagogue looked forward to it, including the reading of the Megillah. During the ceremony we used the gregors as noisemakers to chase away Haman. I went to the Purim parties every year, and, of course, I came dressed as Queen Esther.

Eric Sheinin, pharmaceutical company executive

I went to B'nai Zion every afternoon, after grammar school in the 1950s. Some of my friends went to Temple Mizpah and only had to go twice a week. There was a room at Hebrew school where we could go before class, and if you got there early, they had a boy who supervised us. One time he had some girl up there and they were behind the couch making out. I remember Luba Dubner, who was a teacher, and Rabbi Fisher, and especially Cantor Marantz. What a beautiful voice he had! I remember going for my bar mitzvah lessons and he would help me with my preparations. We would have to sing a part together and somebody said how good a duet it was. I kept thinking about how I was going to get through this because I have such an awful voice. I also remember going to post-Bar Mitzvah Club on Sunday mornings. We would have a service and put on Tefillin and then we would have breakfast. The breakfasts were really good and I always looked forward to them.

The Granada Theatre, c.1950. (Courtesy of the CTA.)

Sr. Ann Ida Gannon, college administrator

I heard my first "talkie" at the Granada in the 1920s. It was brand new, and for a while, someone would play the organ near the screen in the front of the theater. I can remember a song that we used to sing, "Across the fairway, the blossoms over there are telling us, in our way, we'd make a peach of a pair." It was one of the songs in one of the movies, although I don't remember the name of the movie. But we were fascinated by the sound. They would also put the notes and words on the screen, and we would sing with the organ. Those were wonderful days and the Granada was a magnificent theater.

Bob Dauber, creative consultant

We started going to the Granada in the 1950s on Saturday afternoons when we were in seventh or eighth grade. And then, when we got into high school, we started going on Friday nights. In grade school, in particular, we would "pick somebody up," which meant that we would go play "kissy face" with someone up in the balcony. And generally, we met people from other schools. That was how we started to branch out. So, we would meet girls from Kilmer and Field and Rogers and Boone. It was the great melting pot on Saturday afternoons. There was an usher at the Granada with the nickname of "Cuddles." Cuddles was kind of like Barney Fife, because he would talk tough, but never bust anybody in the balcony for screwing around. And one time, a couple of the bad dudes from St. George were there. They decided to dangle Cuddles off of the balcony one Saturday afternoon.

On Friday nights, during high school years, we always had a lot of fun at the Granada. There used to be a plainclothes detective from the Rogers Park station named Officer Stanton who was there on Friday nights. This guy, of course, stood out like a sore thumb. He always wore a fedora and some garish clothes like a green tie with orange frogs, so he would be inconspicuous. But, every Friday night, we would walk in and he would be standing there trying to look like he was undercover. And, every Friday night, we would greet him with, "Good evening, Officer Stanton," and he would frown because his cover had been blown. But, one Friday night, a water gun fight broke out on the first floor. It became pretty raucous in the theater with all the squirt guns. They actually stopped the movie, turned the lights on and started rounding up the troublemakers. They marched a bunch of us out into the lobby, put us up against the wall and started frisking us as if we were in a lineup. One of my buddies turned around, and with his squirt gun, pointed it at Officer Stanton and said, "Okay, up against the wall!" Well, nobody got busted, but we were removed from the Granada for the night.

Scott Simon, broadcaster

I remember going to the Granada in the 1960s when I was attending Senn High School. It was a big old theater and for some reason, I can still remember putting my feet down and having to really apply some energy to my knees and ankles to be able to lift up my shoes that had stuck to all of the stuff on the floor. The theater also had a huge, wide screen and we sometimes saw really bad movies as part of the double features. Like the Riviera and the Uptown, the Granada was quite a theater.

Norman Mark, broadcaster

The Granada Theatre was still open in the 1970s when we were living in Rogers Park. One day, I did a story for the old *Chicago Daily News* about movie palaces, and the Granada was one of them. I was exploring the upstairs level and we got into what was obviously the manager's office. I opened a door that hadn't been opened in a long time and there was a cot, probably a casting couch that the manager had used many years before. When it was built in the 1920s, the Granada Theatre was designed so that you felt you were outside a sultan's palace and when you looked up, they had all those twinkling lights and moving clouds on the ceiling. It was certainly a beautiful movie palace in its heyday.

Bob Dauber, creative consultant

We moved to the area around Devon and Greenview in 1947 when I was seven years old. We played a lot of sports, including street football. When you listen to Bill Cosby do his routine about "run down, take the #4 bus to J Street, and I'll fake the ball to you," that's about how we used to play football on Schreiber Avenue that ran perpendicular to Greenview. We also played a lot of pinners, or lags, or what they called stoop ball in New York. You would slam a ball against the side of a building or a curb, and it became like a line ball game. As we got older, we would play softball and football at the empty lot at Schreiber and Ashland. Later, it became Schreiber Park, but earlier, we would play in that big, empty lot. We would also have some brawls over there after our games, and the Catholic kids used to whip the Jewish kids quite a bit back in those days. That's just how it worked out.

Bill Nellis, union fund secretary

After World War II, the big activity in the Loyola neighborhood on Sunday mornings in summer, after church services at St. Ignatius, was a double-header of sixteen-inch softball. The guys would be certain to have a new, hard softball for each game, and I would describe it as an ethnic or religious game because there were the Catholic guys against the Jewish guys. The game would take place at the south end of Sullivan High School on the gravel field. The game would usually begin at noon on Sundays, and this tradition began around 1946. Both teams had some great players, and they ranged in age from nineteen years old to some guys in their mid 30s and early 40s. Many of the players were World War II veterans, and my uncle, who had been in the Army, organized it in the 1940s. And, the whole idea of that neighborhood softball game expanded so that they played softball just about every night of the summer.

John Grigsby, businessman

I was born in Rogers Park in 1940 and lived on Glenwood, near North Shore and Columbia. It was great to live in the neighborhood. We had a ball field behind the 'El' tracks over on Columbia, and an open park. I guess that the only thing I had to worry about was going up on top of the elevated tracks to retrieve a baseball when anybody hit one to right field. My mother would yell at me to get down off of the tracks if she saw me climbing up there. I also learned to hit a tennis ball against the wall that was on the side of the 'El' tracks.

Harold Ramis, movie actor, director and screenplay writer

When I lived in the Loyola neighborhood of Rogers Park during the '50s and '60s, we were not involved in Little League. I knew that there were kids who played Little League, but we played softball in the schoolyard at Kilmer or at Hayt. We played a lot of fast pitch, which involved throwing a Spaulding pinky ball at a box marked out on a wall. There were all kinds of what were called "ledge" games or pinners, as well as line ball. There were lots of kids who played neighborhood-scale games with variations of hide-and-seek that we called Rolevio; we played buck-buck where a few kids held on to each other and to a tree, and the purpose was to jump on their backs until they fell down. We spent a lot of time playing outside during the summer until it was dark and you could hear the mothers calling from their open windows. And, of course, since the apartments weren't air conditioned, it was necessary to open all the doors and windows and sit out on the front porches or the stoops.

Pushball contest at Loyola University, c.1950. (Courtesy of Loyola University Archives.)

Pushball contest winners marching up Sheridan Road, c.1950. (Courtesy of Loyola University Archives.)

Father Siedenburg, professor, interviewed in October 1927

When I came to Rogers Park for the first time in 1903, on a tour of investigation for a site of the new college, there was nothing but sand, scrub oaks, and bush in the Loyola district. It looks just about like Loyola of that time out around Gary, Indiana, now. Maybe the dunes weren't so high, but the place was bleak, you know, wind-swept and offered plenty of sand. Our committee went up to Wilson Avenue on the 'El', which was as far as the 'El' went then, and from that point we took a buggy on up to Rogers Park. There was no sentiment connected with the selection of the site for the college. The land was cheap and seemed to be a good buy. This particular piece of land was called Hayes Point, maybe because some Captain Hayes settled there in the early days. There was a frame house standing on the south side of Hayes Avenue at the time the land was purchased. But the story about anyone named Loyola landing there isn't true at all. Loyola is the name of the town in northern Spain where St. Ignatius, who was the founder of the Jesuit order, was born.

Frank Hogan, independent school administrator

I was president of the sophomore class at Loyola University and part of the ritual was that freshmen at Loyola had to wear beanies until the pushball contest. Then, if they beat the sophomores they could take them off. They must have beaten us because we threw the class president into the lake in November. They originally held the pushball contest where the Gentile Center is now. It used to be a practice field. South of there was a football stadium that could seat 8,000-10,000 people, as well as an oval for track events. The practice field didn't have much grass on it. It was more of a clay thing. They would hose it down and put the pushball in the middle and the students would go at it until one side won.

When Mundelein was built in 1930, Cardinal Mundelein struck some sort of deal that Loyola students would be men, and Mundelein students would be women. The only women at the Lakeshore campus of Loyola were nursing students, and if a female student wanted to take other courses, she would have to go to the downtown campus. My first year at Loyola was in 1955 and that was when they opened up dormitories on the Lakeshore campus. We didn't have classes with the Mundelein women, but Loyola and Mundelein did share Wilson Hall when it was turned into a student union.

Neil Hartigan, attorney and politician

The major restaurant in the St. Ignatius/Loyola area was Wagtayles. It was a very good restaurant and it was located on Loyola Avenue around the corner and down the block west of Sheridan Road and the 'El' station. They served terrific waffles and pancakes at Wagtayles and it was open from early morning until late at night. I remember going there on numerous occasions with my dad, who was the alderman of the 49th ward, U.S. Congressman Charlie Boyle, and my uncle, Frank Hogan. The older men in the neighborhood would go there to drink coffee, read a newspaper and talk about all kinds of issues of the day. It was the place to eat and be seen in the neighborhood.

Loyola University NCAA 1963 Championship Team with Coach George Ireland, left front. (Courtesy of Loyola University Archives.)

Bill Jauss, journalist

I called the 1963 NCAA National Champion Loyola University Ramblers the last amateur team because the next year Johnny Wooden's teams from UCLA started their long run at this thing. Johnny Wooden played within the rules, so to speak, but there was Sam Gilbert behind the bench and he took care of cars and other little incidentals that the players needed, and it was the start of the modern era. Loyola won by playing only five guys who were all legitimate students at the university and all graduated. Loyola wasn't in any conference in '63 and was independent. On the way to the finals they beat the Ohio Valley Conference champions as well as the Southeastern Conference champions from Mississippi State. That was a controversial game because Mississippi State had to leave the state to avoid an injunction that the state legislature put on playing a game involving mixed races. The year before, in 1962, Loyola of Chicago went down to play Loyola of New Orleans and there was a big brouhaha. The blacks objected to segregated seating at the game, and the establishment down there objected to a game involving mixed races, even between two Catholic schools.

Loyola also beat the Big Ten champion (Illinois), and they went to the Final Four and beat Duke from the Atlantic Coast Conference (ACC), and then Cincinnati, which was the defending champion and had been the #1 team the two previous years. Cincinnati was a giant team and what they did best was to protect leads. Their greatest strength was that there was no shot clock in those days, and if you were ahead, you could just hold the ball, pass it around, and stall. They excelled at stalling and they were fifteen points ahead with ten minutes to play against the helter-skelter team from Loyola. It totally frustrated Loyola, because their game was "run-and-shoot." In fact, one time during that season, a network crew came to Loyola's little gym to film this "crazy, organized confusion" as George Ireland called it. They thought they had a two-day gig, but Loyola went into one of those zones where they just couldn't miss and the film shoot was over in ninety minutes. There was nothing more to film. The director wanted to see a rebound shot, but nobody on Loyola missed a shot.

In the title game for the championship, Loyola couldn't do anything and they were down fifteen points. But they scratched their way back and, I remember it vividly because I wrote a poem about the game and their comeback. It was dramatic, totally unexpected, and completely improbable. When I picked those 150 greatest moments in Chicago sports, I campaigned for the Loyola championship game to be number one because it was just so improbable. You talk about upsets. It was an enormous upset, although I had thought that Loyola had a very good team when the season began. Early in the season, I was at Chicago Stadium sitting with some of the Loyola players at a doubleheader when Cincinnati played the first game against Wichita. One Loyola player looked at another. These were two-time national champions with all of these great players. Miller looked at Harkness, and he said, "We can beat these guys!" Loyola got up to the #2 ranking. It was a perfect match between #1 and #2. Yet, people around the country didn't know who Loyola was. The championship game was played at Freedom Hall in Louisville, Kentucky. George Ireland recalled that he got in a cab during the tournament, and the cab driver said, "What is this Loyal?" "Who is Loyal, and where are they from?" Ireland said, "It's Loyola and they're from Chicago." And, the guy said, "Chicago? Is that the place where they invented the atomic bomb?" He was thinking of the University of Chicago. And, Ireland said, "Boy, he's a pretty erudite cab driver. He knows about the splitting of the atom, but he never heard of Loyola." Loyola University received $25,000 as its share for winning the NCAA National Championship in 1963. This goes along with my theory that Loyola was the last amateur team in sports.

Sr. Ann Ida Gannon, college administrator

I came to Mundelein College in 1951 and I taught there for six years before becoming the president of the college. In those years, we didn't go out a great deal so I don't have strong recollections of the neighborhood. We had close cooperation with Loyola University and our students were able to use their student union that was an old garage. There was also a bus turn-around where Devon becomes Sheridan Road and where they built a Standard Oil station. When I was president, I could have purchased those lots for a very low price, but we just didn't have the money. At the time, you could get off the double-decker bus and transfer to the Sheridan Road bus that went to Howard Street. Across the street from the bus turn-around, there was an old building with a lot of little stores. One of our favorite stores was Fannie May where they sold chocolate candy for $.60 a pound. They would also put out free samples. I remember that under the 'El' at Loyola there was a bakery and a restaurant called En-0-Day Inn that was a hangout for the high school and college students.

Katy Hogan, cafe owner

I first came to Rogers Park from the southwest side in the '50s. My mother would wind up corralling some of her eight kids to make the drive to Mundelein College to visit her college classmate, Sr. Kennelly, who taught chemistry there. As a young woman, I saw Rogers Park as a community and Mundelein as part of that community. When I entered the college in 1968, the neighborhood and the density of the housing and people amazed me. I liked it a lot. Mundelein was a fabulous place and it was very connected to the community and it was extremely hip. Its mission was to educate women of all ages. There was a huge commuter class of students and they were a very important part of the college. The commuters were local women, my age and older, who had decided to complete their degrees at Mundelein. So, the college was ahead of its time.

I remember the late '60s and the moratorium against the War. We called it "Bring The War Home," and in October 1969 we all gathered to talk about the Vietnam War and how it affected our lives in this country, especially women. It was an incredible event and very stirring. It was one of the most important political events in which I ever participated. It was great to be at Mundelein at that time.

David Orr, politician

The late '60s and the '70s were really exciting times to be teaching, from a political point of view, and I was interested in political events, government and history. At that time, Mundelein was a pretty activist place and actually had a strike in 1970. I can remember all the battles, all the tension and all the tears. It was a wonderful learning experience.

I helped start what was called the "Weekend College In Residence" at Mundelein and it was a great program back in the mid-1970s. Mundelein always had older students that returned to college, and sometimes you would have a nineteen-year-old and a thirty-eight-year-old sitting next to each other in class. But, the Weekend College in Residence was targeted for women who were out there in the world someplace -- business, professional, any kind of work -- and wanted to graduate quickly. They would come on a Friday night, and sometimes they would spend all weekend and leave their husband at home with the kids. That way they could cram their coursework in much more quickly. It was a fascinating teaching experience because these people were hungry to learn. Many of them were professionally accomplished, but felt like they needed a degree. I coached a women's football team when I was teaching there. It was a very constructive and supportive atmosphere. I really think that Mundelein put a premium on teaching, unlike the bigger universities.

Freshman class elections at Mundelein College, c.1960. (Courtesy of Mundelein College, Women and Leadership Archives.)

The Morse Avenue Neighborhood

Boundaries:
Pratt Boulevard to Touhy Avenue (S-N)
Lake Michigan to Clark Street (E-W)

At the turn of the twentieth century, the section of Rogers Park that was the Morse Avenue neighborhood was made up of a few scattered houses east of Clark Street and businesses located along Clark and near the Chicago & Northwestern Railroad station. Some of the streets were unpaved and there were numerous stands of oak and birch trees, along with sand and scrub brush east of Clark and swampy land near and along the lakeshore. In 1901, Touhy Avenue, like Ashland Avenue and Sheridan Road, was paved in slag and macadam. A year later, Sheridan became a boulevard with incandescent lights.

In the 1910s, new houses, two-story apartment buildings, and stores began to appear on Pratt Boulevard, Morse, Touhy and Sheridan, as well as the numerous side streets. The major building boom for the Morse Avenue neighborhood, similar to one that occurred in the Loyola and Howard Street neighborhoods, took place in the 1920s.

Norman Poteshman, whose father, Morry, was the owner of Morry's Store for Men at 1438 W. Morse, remembers when his father first went into business. "My dad's store originally opened on Morse in 1929 as Federal Cleaners and Tailors and was originally located just east of Ashland, next to Caswell's." Morry would later expand into the clothing business and eventually move to a new location where he opened Morry's Store for Men. It was a couple of doors west of another Morse Avenue institution, Ashkenaz Restaurant and Delicatessen.

Restaurant owner Sam Ashkenaz opened for business in 1940, and remained at 1432 W. Morse until the late 1970s. The original Ashkenaz Delicatessen was opened on Chicago's West Side in 1910 by Ashkenaz' parents, George and Ida, before being established in Rogers Park. After Ashkenaz had a fire in the early '50s, Ian Levin got a job there as a soda jerk at the newly rebuilt restaurant. "In those days, Ashkenaz was the first place to really give fancy names to positions at restaurants. At thirteen, I became Ashkenaz' first fountain engineer. It was a very busy place, and they used an intercom system as early as 1954. I would have to make sodas and phosphates and sundaes very quickly because of the high volume of customers."

Ashkenaz was the favorite place for neighborhood high school students, especially at lunch, after school and on Friday nights following movies at the Granada Theatre. Ashkenaz also had delicatessen take-out food. When Rick Kogan visited his grandmother, Ida Kogan, at her apartment at Pratt and Ashland, he would often be sent to Ashkenaz "to buy the stuff that my grandmother had forgotten to buy to cook dinner. You know, something like, 'you've got to go over to Ashkenaz because we need three poppy seed bagels.'"

Morse Avenue was home to several religious institutions including the Rogers Park English Evangelical Lutheran Church on Morse at Paulina; St. Jerome Church and School on Paulina between Morse and Lunt; Temple Mizpah, the Reform synagogue just west of Morse and Ashland; and the Congregational Church of Rogers Park on the southeast corner of Morse and Ashland. There was also a Jewish Community Center (JCC) located west of Sheridan on Morse that moved to a new site in a house on the northeast corner of Estes and Greenview in the 1950s.

There were stores, restaurants, pharmacies and apartment-hotels, as well as a bowling alley, pool hall, and the Coed Theatre, all located on Morse from Sheridan to Ashland. One well-remembered place was Caswell's, officially known as the Caswell-Morse Sweet Shop, where one could purchase cigars, newspapers, candy and school supplies. And, as Shecky Greene remembers, "Caswell's was that little school-type store that had great hot dogs, too. I loved the Caswells, and I can picture Mrs. Caswell with her black hair pulled back. They were just wonderful to everyone in the neighborhood."

Among other places on Morse were Ruth Frock Shop, Winsberg Brothers, Morseview Pharmacy, Davidson's Bakery, Dutch Mill Candy, DeMar Restaurant, Ma Gordon's Delicatessen and Home Bakery, Rocky's, Morse "L" Drugs (owned by Ray and Herman Goldenson), John Geroulis' Shoe Repair, located under the 'El' tracks, Froikin's Delicatessen and Knishery, and of course, Kerr's. Accord-

Aerial view of beaches in Rogers Park, 1937. (Courtesy of the Chicago Sun-Times.)

St. Jerome Church banquet, c.1945. Photograph by Henry Green.
(Courtesy of the Chicago Historical Society, ICHi 32258.)

ing to Nancy Rae Goldman, "Kerr's made the absolutely best hamburgers I have ever tasted. And, with one of their milkshakes, it was a meal made in heaven. It was such a little place, but I loved to go there."

The Coed Theatre was popular for many local children. Judy Karpen Flapan remembers paying twelve cents to see double features, cartoons and serials. By the early '50s, the price had increased to a quarter. "It was a whole day's entertainment and the kids would fill the theater every Saturday, make lots of noise, and throw their popcorn boxes and candy at the screen."

Richard Lang recalls other places east of the 'El' tracks. "There was Hilda's, a sort of 'greasy spoon,' where Hilda served hot dogs and hamburgers. It was located near the Morse Avenue Recreation Center at 1308 W. Morse that had a bowling alley and a pool hall. The bowling announcer on television, 'Whispering Joe' Wilson, used to bowl there, and I recall that he was a terrible bowler. In the '50s they had pin boys before the installation of automatic pinsetters. On Sheridan Road, a block south of Morse was the Toddle House where you could get great hamburgers and hash browns from early morning to late at night."

While there weren't many parks nearby, kids in the neighborhood were ingenious in creating street and alley games. Ian Levin used to play with the other children around his apartment building at Estes and Glenwood. "We had street games including a pinners/baseball game where we painted the bases in the streets and alleys. In the winter, we used to have snowball fights with the kids who lived across the street on the south side of Estes."

Edward Mogul grew up on the 1600 block of Estes during the '50s. "I used to play with the O'Donovan brothers who lived in my building. Our time was spent in the back alley that ran from Ashland to Paulina. Peter O'Donovan and I used to play a game where we would stand on opposite sides of the alley, spread our arms against the garages, and fire golf balls at each other. If you flinched, you had to stand there and the other person would fire another golf ball at you. If you didn't flinch, it was your turn to throw one at him. Luckily we didn't cause any brain damage to each other."

The Morse Avenue neighborhood was also home to two grammar schools, one public and one parochial: Field Elementary School on Ashland between Greenleaf and Lunt; and St. Jerome School on Lunt and Paulina, the Catholic elementary school for St. Jerome Parish. Don Pardieck attended St. Jerome School in the '50s and remembers many of his teachers who were a mixture of nuns and lay teachers. They included "my second grade teacher, Sr. Salvatore who had been there for years and years. She was one of the nuns who didn't have a college education, but I learned as much from her as if she had gone to college. My favorite teacher was Sr. Mary Veronique, my seventh grade teacher who was pretty young at that time."

For other students at St. Jerome's, like Joan Wester Anderson and her brother, Jerry Wester, almost all of their teachers were Sisters of Charity of the Blessed Virgin Mary (BVMs). The students would refer to the nuns by a spe-

cial name that reflected both respect and fear, "black veiled monsters." Joan recalls that for several years she had looked forward, with much anticipation, to having Sr. Virginetta for her eighth grade teacher. However, when she finally reached eighth grade, a priest, Fr. Simpson, was assigned to teach her class. He was opposed to the interaction between the boys and girls in sixth and seventh grades. "By that time, we were having parties and playing 'spin the bottle.' But, Fr. Simpson announced that there would be no more boy/girl parties, and that was a major disappointment," said Joan.

Field School students who were Catholic would be excused from their classes around 2:00 p.m. every Wednesday to attend Catechism classes at St. Jerome's. Marilyn Sensendorf can still picture "the nuns walking down the hall behind us on our way to Catechism class; you could hear the rosary beads clicking as they were coming. I remember feeling a sense of terror." Marilyn also recalled "the milk bottles with little cardboard caps that were delivered by the milk boys and girls to the classes. And, I remember the air raid drills in the '50s, when we would go down into the dark and dingy basement, sit on the floor, and put our hands over our heads."

Some kids moved to the neighborhood when they were preteens and attended Field School for sixth, seventh and eighth grades. Shelly Lang Berger moved to Farwell and the lake in 1954 from Chicago's West Side. "It was difficult being eleven years old and moving to a new neighborhood, but I soon made good friends at Field. It helped that my cousin, Ricky,

Top: Rogers Park Public Library, c.1945.
Bottom: Jewish Community Center, c.1955.

Girls at water fountain, Loyola Park, 1950. (Courtesy of the Chicago Park District.)

had been attending the school for several years. I have fond memories of going to fortnightly dances at the Loyola Park field house which I looked forward to because I really loved to dance."

Bobbi Levin Feinstein recalls events related to holidays at Field, like Valentine's Day and Halloween. "I remember decorating the Valentine's Day box in our class and everyone bringing little valentines to give to their classmates. Then, in preparation for Halloween, there was a contest to see who could draw the best pictures and the winners got the opportunity to paint their pictures on the windows of Morse Avenue merchants."

David Schultz spent a lot of time in the schoolyard at Field after school. "There were always choose-up softball games. We would play the games on the gravel and come home with skinned knees and elbows and worn-out gym shoes. We used sixteen-inch softballs, Spaulding tennis balls or pinkies, and we would get these hard rubber balls that had seams on them as if they were real baseballs. And after our softball games we would all go down to Lunt-El Drugstore and get Cokes for a nickel or vanilla Cokes for six cents, without ice."

The beaches, parks and empty lots along the lake were places of great importance in the Morse Avenue neighborhood, from Pratt on the south to Touhy on the north. Roger Cooper remembers when "there was a wooded area on the east side of Sheridan Road that extended from Touhy to Greenleaf for about two blocks. It was a thick woods that was very foreboding. It was removed when they built Loyola Park in 1950."

Joseph Epstein lived at 7023½ N. Sheridan Road. "I can still remember the sound of the Sullivan High School football team practicing behind our apartment building in the park between Lunt and Greenleaf, and Coach Ralph Margolis screaming at his players in Yiddish -- 'schtunk! schtunk!' -- when he was displeased with their performances. Every Sunday morning men would play softball in the park."

In the '40s and '50s, Edward Margolis lived in an apartment building on Farwell that was closest to the lake. "It was a unique place because the park was there and we had access to facilities along the lake. We went swimming at Farwell and Morse Beaches; fishing off of Farwell pier; and played tennis at the courts in the park. The Park also had a hill where we would go sledding in winter. There was a World War I cannon on that hill, so we called it 'Cannon Hill'."

Gail Gordon remembers ice-skating every day after grade school at Touhy Beach. "There was a little stand that sold hot chocolate and hot tamales. And, in the summer, we bought frozen Snickers bars. In high school we would go to Morse Beach, sit on the grass and flirt with the guys, who were usually much too busy with their poker games." Lynn Ressman Simon-Lodwick recalls going to Greenleaf Beach in the summers when she was in grammar school. "The mothers would play cards and the grandfathers would play pinochle, and sometimes chess and checkers. It was a family atmosphere with everybody spending their time swimming and getting sun-burned."

Sue Sosin recalls that "in the '50s and

Hi! Neighbor Parade on Sheridan near Morse, 1965. Photograph by Ralph Arvidson. (Courtesy of the Chicago Sun-Times.)

Easter Parade on Clark, 1989.

'60s we spent almost every summer weekend at the beach. There was a hierarchy among the Jewish kids in those days, with the high school kids hanging out at Farwell Beach, or as we used to call it, 'Farfel' beach, and the college kids at Morse beach. Of course, the high school girls would walk to Morse to check out the college guys, and flirt with them."

For Donna Price Greenberg, the beaches in the summer meant "getting hot dogs at the little stands at Morse, Lunt and Greenleaf, and hanging out at the beaches. When we were old enough to drive, we would take our cars and whip the corners at the ends of the streets by the beaches. Once my car had vapor lock and stalled out while I was 'whipping' around the turn at Morse, and that was quite embarrassing."

The Rogers Park Library was one of the favorite places for residents of the Morse Avenue neighborhood, and Ms. Dorothea Federgren was everyone's favorite librarian. When children were looking for new books to read, Ms. Federgren would walk them through the library to help select books that fit their interests.

There were the many drugstores, most with soda fountains, throughout the neighborhood, including Mitchell Jacob's Lunt-El Drug Store, Lutz Pharmacy at 7043 N. Glenwood, Mesirow-Sheridan Drugs at 6800 N. Sheridan, West Pharmacy at 7001 N. Sheridan, and Touhy Pharmacy at Touhy and Clark.

By the 1970s, the neighborhood had begun to change from a heavy Jewish population to one with a broader mix of ethnic, racial and religious groups, and through the 1980s and 1990s, major changes occurred. However, Katy Hogan, co-owner of the Heartland Cafe on Lunt and Glenwood feels that "the neighborhood has aged well. I think that the significant thing has been the success of independent politics in 1979 with the election of David Orr as 49th Ward Alderman. I agree with the idea of Section 8 subsidized housing. It brings people together who are willing to be together. This neighborhood is moving toward becoming the paradise I hope to live in, where everybody lives together and where we overcome the barriers."

Michael James, Katy's partner at the Heartland Cafe notes that he "always saw the neighborhood as interesting because there were a lot of different people. Early on, when I first came here in the late '60s, there were a lot of Catholics, Jews and student-types. Then, the Jews tended to move west and people would talk about how the neighborhood was going 'down.' That perception was based on the fact that more African-Americans, Hispanics, and poorer people were moving into the apartments and houses, but I have always rooted for people of color and for diversity. I am pleased that Rogers Park is the most diverse neighborhood in the city, and maybe in the country.

"As the neighborhood improves and more people begin moving in and coming back, I think that the Morse neighborhood will keep getting better and better. To me that means being more international, diverse and interesting."

Heartland Cafe, 12:00 am, January 1, 2000. Photograph by Wally Reichert.

Birch forest at Lunt and Ashland, c.1900.

Rogers Park News Herald, **June 29, 1900**

At the rate the native birch trees are dying out on the east side where formerly such fine groves existed, it will not be a great while before all will be gone.

Sr. Ann Ida Gannon, college administrator

In 1919, we lived in Rogers Park at 6928 N. Lakewood, near Morse Avenue. There was an apartment house at Morse and Lakewood and we lived right next to it. Rogers Park was a very simple, family-oriented neighborhood and I remember Morse Avenue as being a tree-lined, quiet street. Mr. Geery, who was our grocer, lived next door to us and his grocery store was on Morse, west of Wayne. Across the street, east of the elevated trains, were tennis courts that were turned into ice skating rinks during the winter. The A&P was there along with mostly family-owned stores. I went to St. Jerome School at Morse and Paulina. Also on Morse were a Piggly Wiggly, some apartment buildings and homes, and many birch trees. The street was nothing like it is today.

Dr. Ward Green Klarke, interviewed in November 1927

While I did not come to Rogers Park to live until 1906, I remember coming to the district as early as 1884 to hunt. Ducks found Rogers Park a good lighting place and we came here for the excellent hunting to be found. At that time there were no cross streets between Pratt and Touhy Avenues. I remember when Carter Harrison was mayor and Sheridan Road was improved from a sandy stretch to a cinder path. That was in 1894 and the time of the bicycle craze, and people riding their bikes used to venture north of Devon Avenue because the wooded land was beautiful. Then the Birchwood District was covered with white birch and now you cannot find one in the whole of Rogers Park.

Looking north on Ashland at Pratt, c.1940. (Courtesy of the CTA.)

Congregational Church of Rogers Park day camp, c.1940. Photograph by Henry Green. (Courtesy of the Chicago Historical Society, ICHi 25618.)

Judy Karpen Flapan, retiree

At Morse and Ashland, on the southeast corner, there was the Congregational Church where my girl scout troop met and I took dancing lessons. Across the street, on the northeast corner, was Caswell's where we would shop for our school supplies. Then, on the north side of the street was Winsberg Brothers, which had lots of dry goods. There was Leonard's, a children's clothing store. There were so many stores on Morse Avenue, when I was growing up in the '40s and '50s, that the mothers didn't have to go anyplace out of the neighborhood for their shopping. There were grocery stores and bakeries. I can remember Davidson's located east of Ashkenaz, and Becker's near Morse and Greenview.

Howard Schein, university administrator

There was this store on Morse and Lakewood that was kind of like Caswell's on Morse and Ashland. It was a place on the way to school where everybody would stop to buy school supplies and candy and stuff like that. It was called Jack's, or at least that's what we called it because there was this guy named Jack who owned it.

There was a lot of activity on Morse when I was growing up in the '50s. There were a couple of clothing stores, there was always Ashkenaz, and there was a delicatessen east of Glenwood called Jacob's that had a meat market and a delicatessen. Across the street, on the south side of Morse, east of Glenwood, was a gas station and a kosher butcher with cages of live chickens in the window. You would go into the butcher and he would kill the chickens, on the spot, to fill your order. On the north side of the street, east of Glenwood, was Fine's Meat Market and the Coed Theatre. I have special memories about the Coed because they had Saturday matinees for only $.12 admission, with those serialized cliffhangers. And, every once in a while, I think the Field PTA would sponsor free movies at the Coed. Later on, the Coed closed and the building became an Orthodox Jewish synagogue.

Donna Price Greenberg, businesswoman

I would walk to Morse Avenue by going south on Glenwood. I remember the Coed Theatre that later became a synagogue, and that was where my grandmother used to go to shul. Next to it was the bowling alley where my father bowled, and the pool hall. And, then, there was a tire place that I think was Duxler's Tires. The JCC was further east toward the Town House that was on the southeast corner of Morse and Sheridan. As you would go west from Glenwood, under the 'El', there was Geroulis' Shoe Repair and Manny's Drugs. On the north side of the street, west of the 'El', was DeMar's, Davidson's, Froikin's Knishery, a record store, Top Hat Liquor Store, Woolworth's, Ashkenaz, Morry's Store for Men, and then Dutch Mill Candies. Across Greenview, were Morseview Pharmacy and the Haliburton Hotel. Going down Morse, towards Ashland, there was Leonard's Children's Store, Winsberg Brothers, Ruth Frock Shop and Caswell's at the corner. On the south side of Morse, I remember Rocky's, Kerr's, a hardware store, Turner's Men's Store, and Jacobson's Drugstore at the southwest corner of Morse and Glenwood. Morse Avenue was just the place for everything.

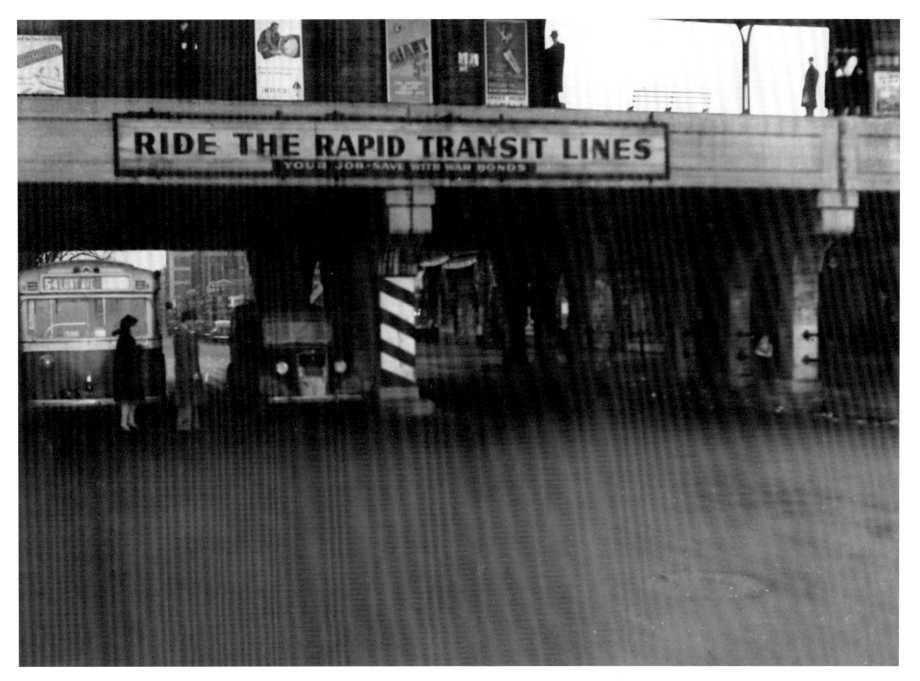

Morse Avenue Elevated Train Station, c.1940. (Courtesy of the Chicago Historical Society, ICHi 32279.)

Empty lots at the corner of Touhy and Sheridan, c.1945. (Courtesy of the Chicago Park District.)

Marilyn Sensendorf, secretary

I remember the empty lots on the west side of Sheridan Road at Estes, Greenleaf and Touhy. We played baseball and all sorts of other games in those empty lots in the 1940s even though they were weed-infested. We would constantly get chiggers all over our socks from playing in there.

Ian Levin, judge

Before they ever built Loyola Park, the whole area from Greenleaf to Touhy used to be empty lots and hills. In the winter, we used to sled down those hills, right up to the edge of Lake Michigan, and sometimes into the lake. So, I clearly remember it when it was vacant land, and before it was a park.

Bobbi Levin Feinstein, event planner

There was an empty lot on Estes and Sheridan before they built the apartment buildings and there were billboards there. We would build forts alongside and inside the billboards. My mother didn't want me to go there because she thought it was dangerous. But we would climb up the back of the billboards where there was a trap door, and we just thought that it was the neatest thing. My mother would discover that I had been playing there because the stickers from the weeds would become attached to my socks. I have such fond memories of playing in those empty lots.

Edward Mogul, attorney and educator

In the '50s, when my childhood exploration of the world expanded beyond the alley behind my home on Estes Avenue, I made it over to the fire station which was one block south on Greenleaf, and half a block west of Paulina. I remember, as a small child, going over and squatting down on the edge of the goldfish pond that the firemen maintained right next to the station on the alley. I was fascinated looking at the fish and the way they had constructed buildings in the pond that made it kind of a city for fish. I was transfixed by the world that they had built. Obviously it was something that a child would find attractive, but it also was probably something that helped them pass the time of day. I never really talked much to the firemen, but I do remember going into the fire station once. It was very well-maintained and I recall how gleaming and clean it was. I liked how open the fire station was. It seemed that the door was always open and I don't remember ever seeing it closed. It not only represented an excursion out of my alley, but it also represented a step towards contacts with a greater world, an expansion of my universe that I called my neighborhood.

Nancy Rae Goldman, artist

There was a fire station on Greenleaf near Clark and they had the cutest little fishpond. One time, when I was a little kid, I went by there and they were giving away turtles. So, I dragged this little turtle home in a bucket and every cat in the neighborhood followed me. Needless to say, my mother forced me to take the turtle back to the fire station because, as I remember, she felt that the turtle was too big to be in our apartment. I do remember dawdling at the station on a regular basis, looking at the fish, the fire engines and the Dalmation dog that the firemen kept there.

Jerry Wester, grammar school educator

I used to go to the fire station on Greenleaf, east of Clark, when I was growing up. It was near the library, and I liked to go to the station to watch the fish in the pond that the firemen had built alongside the station, next to the alley. One time, the firemen allowed me to come inside and one of them took me down the fire pole and let me sit in the driver's seat on the fire truck. I remember those shiny metal poles that they would slide down from the second floor and how clean they kept the fire station. They also had a beautiful black and white Dalmatian that was always sitting in front of the station. It was a wonderful experience being there as a young boy.

Miniature garden at fire station, 1723 W. Greenleaf, c.1945. Photograph by Henry Green. (Courtesy of the Chicago Historical Society, ICHi 25621.)

Site for new apartment buildings, 1130 W. Lunt, 1947. Photograph by Hedrich-Blessing. (Courtesy of the Chicago Historical Society, HB-09856A.)

Field School PTA pageant, 1947. Photograph by Henry Green. (Courtesy of the Chicago Historical Society, ICHi 32292.)

Field School clean-up program, 1947. Photograph by Henry Green. (Courtesy of the Chicago Historical Society, ICHi 32288.)

David Schultz, attorney

Field School was this "heaven," and I have marvelous recollections of my years attending there in the '50s. We were all very high-achieving students in the Schultz family. My sister, Sharon, was a world-beater and spelling champ, and so was my other sister, Maxine. Then, I came to Field, and the teachers figured, "Oh, here's another Schultz kid." I think that the three of us won every spelling bee for six years in a row.

As for the teachers, I started with Mrs. Linden, who seemed like she was one hundred years old when she was our kindergarten teacher. She was a sweet, kindly grandmotherly kind of woman who was a real throwback to the early days of teaching. In third or fourth grade, there was Ms. Valerio, who was my favorite teacher. She was just wonderful and was well-rounded, very intelligent and very supportive. And in eighth grade, I had Mrs. Schumacher, who was a terrific teacher and was very strong in her knowledge of Chicago and American history. I also remember Mr. Frankel, the gym teacher, who used to grab the guys by the collar and kind of toss them around in a rough way if they weren't towing the line. And then, there was Ms. Julia C. Ness, the principal, who was a strong, female figure and who was clearly the boss of the school. Overall, Field School was a wonderful experience.

Marilyn Sensendorf, secretary

I went to Field School beginning in the second grade, and I graduated there in 1956. The make-up of our class was unique because, generally speaking, I think that my sister and I were the only non-Jewish kids in our classes at Field. So, we were usually among a small group of kids who were in school on the Jewish holy days. We went to St. Jerome's over on Lunt Avenue for our catechism class every Wednesday afternoon. As a younger child, the fact that I was Catholic and went to Field School didn't bother me. In fact, I didn't notice the difference at all until I got older and had a Jewish boyfriend. I must have been about twelve and he was thirteen, because I went to his bar mitzvah. At that point, his mother told him not to go out with non-Jewish girls, and that's when I became very aware of the differences. And, I do remember the teachers at Field, including Bromley, Wilkenning, DeGerald, Smith and Monaghan. Mrs. Monaghan taught home economics and we would have to cook in that class. The principal, Julia C. Ness, would have to eat what we cooked and try out all of our food.

Howard Schein, university administrator

I liked Field School a lot, and I really don't have any bad memories of it. I remember that when we went to first grade in the early '50s, there were two tiers of teachers. There were the old ones and the new ones. The older women teachers were ones who may have been spinsters and who wore those black shoes with big heels and were pretty tough disciplinarians. I remember a teacher in the room next door to us who would put kids in the garbage can as punishment, and sometimes lock them in the coat closet. My teachers never did that. The younger ones were on their first teaching assignment, and a few of them were quite attractive.

I remember the focus on learning the alphabet and phonics, and we seemed to do that everyday in first grade. We loved recess and our main game was to play "pom pom." Every once in a while, the kids would play marbles in the gravel schoolyard. It was a game called "pots" where we would dig little holes and shoot our marbles from hole to hole. And, frequently the Duncan yo-yo man would come to the schoolyard and demonstrate how to use yo-yos.

Detectives at Rogers Park police station, 1946. Photograph by Henry Green. (Courtesy of the Chicago Historical Society, ICHi 32269.)

Resident of West Rogers Park neighborhood, 1940s-1960s

I was briefly abducted as a kid, and the guy wound up taking me to the brickyards. It was Halloween night, and I was trying to tag along with my older brother while he was trick-or-treating. He had gone ahead with his friends, and I found myself standing alone on a corner near my home. I could see a man walking toward me and then he asked me if I was lost and if I needed any help. I told him that my brother wouldn't let me come with him, so the man offered to walk with me. But, instead of taking me trick-or-treating, he took me to the brickyards and, once we were there, I realized that he might hurt me. So I had the foresight to get away and run home. I told my parents, who quickly called the police, and they caught him. But, from then on, my family had a changed sense of security about the neighborhood and we began locking the doors when we went out.

Resident of Loyola neighborhood, 1940s-1950s

There was a great sense of neighborhood and it was safe. However, I'll tell you one funny thing that I remember. We always had live-in help until I went to grammar school. My mother used to get farm girls who would live in our house, take care of us, baby-sit and serve as maids. One time my sister and I opened up the maid's suitcase and discovered a gun. When she found out, she told us that if we ever told our parents about the gun, she would shoot us. We were so petrified of her that we never revealed her secret to our parents.

Resident of Howard neighborhood, 1940s-1950s

A whole bunch of us used to hang out around Noskin's Pharmacy on Jarvis. I was probably in my freshman year in high school, and a group of us, including some older kids, were sort of fooling around and shoplifting and hanging around the store. We were going in and out of the pharmacy and doing just dumb, kid stuff, but we were definitely stealing and we got caught. Well, the pharmacist called the police who came out and took us to the station and called our parents. It scared the heck out of me and that was pretty much the end of my shoplifting days.

Shecky Greene, comedian

Touhy Beach was across Sheridan Road from my apartment. At the beach there was the little gym that was part of Sam Leone's place. The gym was famous because of the way it was designed and the low ceiling at one end. You had to shoot the basketball low or it would hit the ceiling. When I was a lifeguard at Sam Leone's Touhy Beach in the 1940s, I would spend a lot of time at the lifeguard station with the other guys. During the winter we would ice-skate there, and, in the summer, we would play softball. Many years after I had moved out of Rogers Park, I came back to honor Sam Leone at a party for him at the American Legion hall on Devon. I was singing to him when I remember that Sam couldn't hear a thing. He was almost deaf. But, I loved being there and seeing everyone and honoring Sam. There was a man that really loved his job, and he loved the kids, and I think that if they didn't pay him at all, he still would have done that job.

Howard Schein, university administrator

Every nice evening in the summer during the '50s, Sam Leone would take us water skiing. After dinner, the kids would come down to the beach and get into the big crew boat and row it a couple of hundred yards off shore and anchor it. Then, Sam would pull us behind his speedboat and we would water ski until it got dark. Sam made all of the skis. One of his glories was towing twelve kids at a time. He had a rope with two yokes on it and each yoke had six ski lines so we could spread apart a lot. Then he would get a couple of lifeguards in motorboats to trail us, so that if you fell, you would just get picked up and they didn't have to stop the whole thing. We did these marathons, and there were times when we would ski all the way downtown, twelve at a time.

At the end of the regular lifeguard season, Sam Leone would take a group of lifeguards on a Canadian canoe trip and this was an annual ritual. They took all the canoes that were at Touhy Beach that he had made. They had a camping trailer that Sam had built that looked like the Woody station wagon and he would tow it behind. The camping trailer carried all the equipment and the center of the trailer had a big, metal pole that would serve as the center pole of a large tent. The trailer would also serve as a chuck wagon. Once, instead of going to Canada, we went to Washington, DC, and we camped out in a trailer park there. The following year, he took a group of kids down to Florida for spring break and we camped out at a trailer park and went deep-sea fishing. Mr. Miller, who owned Miller's Steak House, also owned a charter boat in Florida and he gave us a free day on the boat. Sam just wanted to take the lifeguards on a great trip.

Ian Levin, judge

We lived about two blocks from Touhy Beach and we used to play basketball at the little gym. It was almost like a barn. On one side of the gym, the ceiling was right at the level of the basket and on the other side, there were all these pipes. I nicknamed that gym "the Jungle," because in the wintertime there was no heat, and it seemed like an indoor/outdoor gym because it would be as cold as thirty degrees in the winter. Sam Leone was responsible for Touhy Beach and was very famous in the neighborhood and throughout the city. He loved the kids. I have this memory of when we were about ten years old in the early '50s. They had built a beautiful new park and field house at Loyola Park that was adjacent to Touhy Beach. People began gravitating to the new park, including myself, because they had modern facilities. I think that Sam took it very personal and he was hurt by it.

Sam Leone at Touhy Beach, c.1950. Photograph by Ed DeLuga. (Courtesy of Chicago Sun-Times.)

Sam Leone is thanked by the Hodge family after rescue, c.1950. (Courtesy of the Chicago Sun-Times.)

Children playing at Loyola Beach, 1950. (Courtesy of the Chicago Park District.)

Sunbathers at Loyola Beach, c.1950. (Courtesy of the Chicago Park District.)

Gordon Segal, business owner

One early spring in the '40s, I went with a friend down to the lake when the ice was beginning to break up. We went to the bottom of Sheridan Road, where it turns, right by Loyola University, climbed over the rocks there and constructed a little cave along the beach. We built a fire with some driftwood, and with the lake on one side, and the beating waves, we sat inside this cave-like structure that we had created. We stayed there until late in the day, and our parents didn't know where we had gone. After it got dark, they became very worried. I remember that experience because we used to do a lot of adventuresome trips in those days. I also remember going to Farwell Beach. As a kid, I used to go to the pier and fish for perch, and I remember that we used to fish either with rods, or we had trolls that had four or five hooks on them. Then, of course, we would go to Farwell Beach and look at all the girls. But, the beach was ruined in the '50s during the Korean War when the Army took it over and built an anti-aircraft emplacement. The Army had a base there during the war, and they used to march down Glenwood and sing Army songs, in cadence.

Richard Lang, college educator

One of my earliest memories of Morse Beach was that, during the 1950s, there was some kind of Army base that was built on the beach with an anti-aircraft battery. The base was inside a barbed wire fence, and the kids could walk up to the fence and watch the soldiers on duty. They used to play baseball and fast pitch on the base and we would watch them. So if you had nothing to do you could watch the soldiers. I also remember that at the end of Morse, on the south side of the street, was what we called the "empty lot." Now it's a sculpted park, but when I was six years old, it was like a jungle. It was hilly and it had trees, and we used to build tree forts as well as underground forts.

Bob Berman, farmer

One day during the summer when I was six years old, my mother took my five-year old neighbor, Benny, and me to Albion Beach, just a short walk from my home. Once we got there, I decided it would be fun if both of us tried to find my little brother who was attending day camp at Loyola Park. Without telling my mother, we started the long walk north, but once at Loyola Park, we couldn't find anyone who knew my brother. After a while we gave up and headed back to Albion. When we were about halfway back, an older boy of eleven or twelve came running up to us and asked if I was Bob Berman. I said, yes, and he told me to come quickly with him back to Albion. There were fire trucks, a scuba team, and, in the middle of it all, my hysterical mother, who thought that we had drowned. I guess I was lucky that I didn't get a spanking that night from my father, but my parents were so glad that I was all right that it took their minds off any punishment.

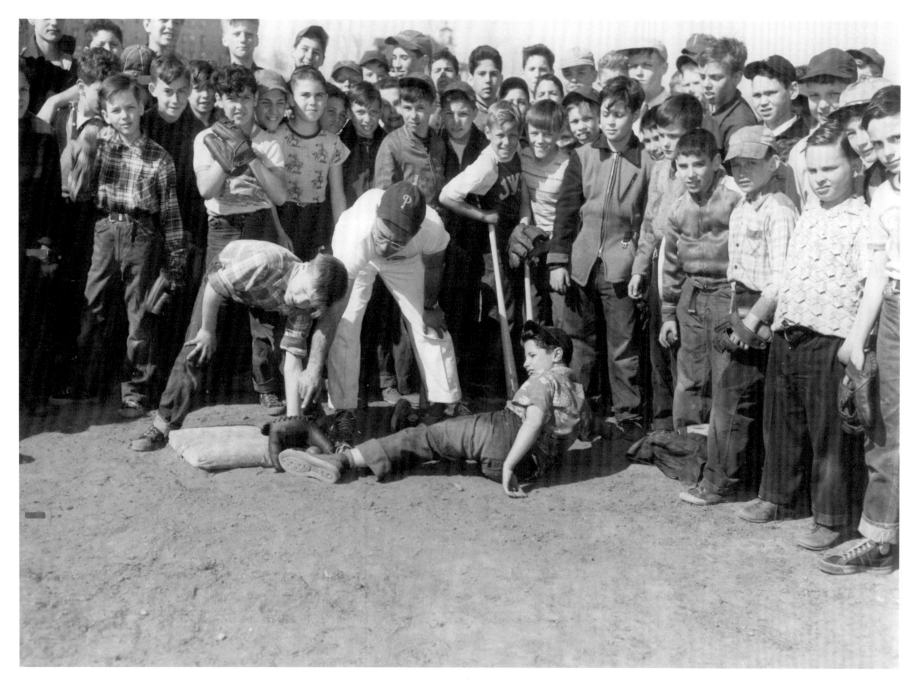

Loyola Park baseball practice, c.1950. (Courtesy of the Chicago Park District.)

Curly Waller, Letter To The Editor, *Rogers Park News* 1930

Softball! My heart bleeds when I see it. Where's the low curve on the outside corner, the high hard one, the stolen base and above all, what happened to that wonderful sound -- the sharp crack when bat meets ball in baseball? But that never, ever happens in this inane substitute game called softball! And, what if you become proficient in this softball game? You get a contract paying you the magnificent sum of $300 a year with the Cheezy Cheese company's "Yellow Coats." You play short-center. Is it a position or a description? I say it's time to call a halt. Let Chicago go back to the American game we all love -- baseball. When spring comes and the boys meet after school in the playground, let the park instructor hand them a baseball, not an imitation melon, and Chicago will once more bring forth the baseball progeny it was so proud of in years gone by.

Ian Levin, judge

I have very fond memories of Touhy Beach because I used to play baseball there all the time at their little field down by the lake. If you were a left-handed batter, it was easy to hit the ball into the lake. On Sundays, there used to be big choose-up games of teams that were made up of Gentiles and Jews. I used to go there with my dad and either watch or play in those games in the late '40s and early '50s. Later on, I played for the Touhy Midgets, and we would play against teams from other city parks. We had a very good team, and one time we participated in the Bud Billiken Tournament that included mostly teams of black kids from Chicago's South Side. Our team did very well and we went all the way to the championship game. I was pitching, and I got really psyched up for the big game. Well, I wound up and threw the ball so fast that I beaned a black kid from the other team. I thought that my life was going to end, since we were a white team in a black neighborhood. But, nothing happened and we did win the championship.

David Schultz, attorney

My older sister, Sharon, became an early fixture at Touhy Beach. She was a tomboy, and, in fact, she broke the gender line for lifeguards at the beach, working for Sam Leone. Sam was a real tough guy, but Sharon was persistent and bull-headed in her younger days. She would not be denied and, in the '50s, she became a lifeguard there, hung out with the other lifeguards, and did all the rough and tumble stuff that the boys did. However, that was not the life for me, and I had no interest to go out on boats, and tie knots and do all those scouting-type things. So, I was always more comfortable playing ball down at Estes and Greenleaf and at the Loyola Field House.

Dance practice at Loyola Park Field House, c.1950. (Courtesy of the Chicago Park District.)

Dance recital at Loyola Park Field House, c.1950. (Courtesy of the Chicago Park District.)

Patrons in booth at Ashkenaz Restaurant, 1967. Photograph by Ed Jarecki. (Courtesy of the Chicago Sun-Times.)

Shecky Greene, comedian

Ashkenaz was the first place I knew where they said, "Grrab ah teecket." And I'd say, I was number one, and the guy would say, "Too late, ve're closed." That was their sense of humor. At Ashkenaz, I always remember the one waitress there who had everything on her dress, and one day I said to her, "Why don't you just put it in hot water and give me the soup?" She just laughed. There was never the "New York attitude" at Ashkenaz. It was that small town attitude, like if you made a joke, they laughed, and they went along with you. Sam Ashkenaz and Dorothy and all of them were very close friends of ours, you know, because that's when we all became friendly. And even when I got into show business, they were all following my career. The whole neighborhood followed my career, and it was such a great feeling to have support from the people that I had known from the time I was a kid.

Edward Mogul, attorney and educator

The high point for family socializing in the '50s would be to go to Ashkenaz during the heat and mugginess of the summer. We would line up outside, just waiting to get inside and be in the cool of their air conditioning. You wouldn't mind waiting outside because Sam and Cal ran that place like a military operation, busing the tables themselves, and quickly getting people in and out of the restaurant. You would also be able to see your neighbors inside and outside Ashkenaz. And, of course, the food was fantastic. My father liked to eat, and he was a big man in many ways. I remember once watching as he ate a boiled beef flanken in a pot. They brought out this gleaming, stainless steel kettle that must have been a foot-and-a-half tall. Floating in the kettle were beef, a whole corn, a couple of potatoes, noodles, and so on. It would take an hour-and-a-half for him to digest the meal. The service there was normally very, very efficient. But once, I remember that it was so slow that my father became impatient, got up and said, "What is this, a bus station or something?" We tried to slide under the table.

In Ashkenaz, people expressed themselves. I remember that when you came in there it was a very narrow storefront, and, when you got in the door you still weren't at your table. You had to wait in line against the wall. But, you were already being treated to the smells and sounds of all the activity. Ashkenaz was our Moulin Rouge, and I think that it really was a wonderful place that's etched into the memories of every person who lived in East Rogers Park. I have heard that, on Sundays, people would come to Ashkenaz from as far away as Wisconsin. It was truly an authentic institution and delicatessen.

Joel Weisman, attorney and broadcaster

We went to Ashkenaz some days after high school in the late '50s. I couldn't really go very often because I was working all the time, but a lot of my friends went there regularly. And my friend Jerry Hirsch used to sit in Ashkenaz and make fun of the waitresses. Any time we would get a bill he'd call out, "Waitress...I demand to see the waitress...get the waitress over here!" And the waitress would come, and Jerry would say, "There's a mistake on this bill and you know it!" Her response was, "What's the matter with the bill?" And Jerry answered, "Nobody ordered this tax! Did anybody order this tax? Did you order this tax?" He would drive them absolutely nuts. And we would sit in Ashkenaz for hours on end, drinking a Coke, and every half an hour somebody would buy an order of French fries, or something, and my friends would argue about who would have to pay for it.

Scott Simon, broadcaster

I went to Ashkenaz many times over the years. I sure remember the picture of Kenny Holtzman, the Chicago Cubs' pitcher, hanging over the Halavah. He appeared to be a "blessed figure" there, although I don't know how many times he had actually visited the restaurant. I can remember sitting there with my friends and having the manager of Ashkenaz lean over and tell us about the last time Kenny Holtzman was in. It seems to me that the story was repeated on a regular basis. But, in any event, you know he was in there at least once because Holtzman had autographed the picture. Since Sandy Koufax had retired by then, Kenny was certainly the best Jewish ballplayer at that time, and could be considered the second best Jewish left-handed pitcher of all time.

Janie Friedman Isackson, college educator

It seemed like we lived at Ashkenaz in the '50s. When I attended Sullivan, we met at the restaurant for breakfast, either before or after student council meetings. We would often go there for lunch, and, we also went there after school. Since I baby sat for my nephew, I would regularly go home to West Rogers Park, pick him up and bring him back to Ashkenaz so that I could spend more time there with my friends. In the summer of our sophomore year, I remember going to Morse Beach almost every day and then walking to Ashkenaz for cheeseburgers, fries and a Coke. Of course, Ashkenaz was THE place to be on Friday nights after going to the Granada.

Sam Ashkenaz, 1976. Photograph by Ed Jarecki. (Courtesy of the Chicago Sun-Times.)

Morse and Glenwood, 1978. Photograph by R. B. Leffingwell. (Courtesy of the Chicago Sun-Times.)

Edward Mogul, attorney and educator

I loved Kerr's, and the secret to their delicious hamburgers was the quarter of a stick of butter that they put on each one. Those were really wonderful hamburgers and Mrs. Kerr was there with her husband, and they kind of took an interest in all of the kids.

On the southwest corner of Morse and Glenwood, I had my first job at the Goldenson Brothers' Drugstore. It became the spawning ground of many a Sullivanite who later became a pharmacist. I remember that I lied to the Goldensons about my age in order to work there. I'm sure that they knew that I wasn't sixteen, but they still hired me. One of my jobs was to work at the soda fountain and I was supposed to make Coca-Cola by mixing one part of syrup to three parts of seltzer water. But I wanted to make it a bit stronger because I liked it that way myself. So, I used to mix it stronger just to see people's teeth smoke, and it was wonderfully rich. I also remember once when I was unloading a package in the front of the store, and shouting back to Ray Goldenson, with the store full of customers, "Ray, what do I do with these Four X Skins?" I didn't know what they were, and he came running out from the back and said, "I'll do that."

Art Berman, attorney and politician

Back in 1976, when I was a candidate in the Democratic primary for State Senate, I got a call from my good friend, Neil Hartigan, who was the Democratic Committeeman of the 49th Ward. And he said, "Art, I know that you are campaigning and have a hot contest, and that you are a great campaigner. I'm wondering if you have the time to help a fellow that I want to help who is also campaigning?" I said, "Sure, Neil, what do you want me to do?" He said, "I'll tell you who he is. His name is Jimmy Carter and he's running for President of the United States and I want to show him how we do campaigning in Chicago." So, I agreed to have Governor Carter join me at the Morse Avenue 'El' platform one morning in March of 1976. At about 6:30 that morning, a limousine pulls up and Neil Hartigan gets out and introduces me to Jimmy Carter. And I said, "Governor, it's nice to meet you and I'm pleased that you are joining me while I meet and greet commuters on their way downtown to work. You'll see lots of people from Rogers Park and you will have the chance to meet them and be introduced." He said, "Art, that sounds terrific, and I'm excited to do it." And that's what we did for the next couple of hours. I'm proud to say that working the voters on the Morse Avenue 'El' platform helped elect the next President of the United States.

But the story gets even better. When we were done working that crowd, I said to Jimmy Carter, "Come on, we're going to go down the street and visit a very popular restaurant." It was about 8:30, so Ashkenaz was still very busy. So, we went in and I showed him how to work the restaurant, and we went from table to table and I introduced Jimmy Carter to everybody who was having breakfast that day. After we were done, we sat down and I ordered lox and bagels for Governor Carter so that he would understand what it meant to be at a Jewish delicatessen.

Marshall Dermer, university educator

In addition to Ashkenaz on Morse Avenue, there was Froikin's that was owned by Sam Froikin. I certainly remember their latkes piled up high on trays on top of the counter where you would order your food. There were also various small shops where the feature food was Vienna hot dogs, and Hilda Franklin owned one of the hot dog places called Hilda's. Rocky's was across the street from Ashkenaz, to the east of Kerr's. Then, at Glenwood and Morse, on the northwest corner, there was DeMars. And, I remember Meyer's Cigar Store, near DeMars. They sold everything there, and when I got seduced into smoking a pipe, that was the place I went for my first pipe and tobacco.

Michael James, cafe owner

In August 2001, the Heartland Cafe celebrated its 25th Anniversary. Our inspiration for opening the Heartland in 1976 came from a million joints from coast to coast and in most of the lower forty-eight right down to Mexico. In October 1975, I met my business partner, Katy Hogan, at a meeting at the Midland Hotel. Along with my former wife, Stormy Brown, we decided to open a wholesome foods restaurant, as part of what we envisioned would be an interconnecting network of businesses to serve the people and build a progressive base in the community. My friend, Jack Bornoff, told me that Lackey's Steak House at Lunt and Glenwood in Rogers Park had closed and the space was available for rent. We checked out the spot on a rainy day and realized that all the 'El' trains stopped there and that the big sidewalk would make a wonderful outdoor cafe.

The Heartland Cafe was intended to be a place where everyone was welcome, a place where you could eat macro (no dairy, no meat), or as "clean and healthy" as you wanted, yet could also come and be with friends and family who might be into the wholesome food thing. While we've been too radical for some and too capitalist for others, too healthy a joint or not pure enough, we obviously include a big enough chunk of everything to keep bringing folks back time and again. We wanted to be a part of the community and Rogers Park is perhaps the most diverse place in America with a rich mix of folks from many racial and ethnic backgrounds. We remain firmly committed to improving our neighborhood in a manner that is first, last, and always, inclusive.

Brian Kozin, former cafe owner

I bought the No Exit in 1983. After we got the place renovated and had our inspection to open it up, the fire inspector told me, "You did a smart thing because East Rogers Park is going to turn around in another two or three years." Well, that was almost twenty years ago, and the neighborhood hasn't completed that turnaround. There are still winos on the street and crack dealers on the corners. And, I'll tell you, it seemed that the police were remarkably lackadaisical about enforcing any kind of law whatsoever. They seemed to take the attitude that they were seeking to just keep a lid on the neighborhood. It is my viewpoint that despite the efforts on the part of some of the developers, they couldn't trash East Rogers Park because it's just too nice of a neighborhood. People just won't leave, regardless of the crime or the perceived crime or danger.

A lot of people stayed and that's why we stayed at the No Exit for all those years making less and less money as the neighborhood seemed to get worse and worse. Our customer base moved out of the neighborhood and only people who had a lot of money and who bought co-ops along the lake stayed, along with the influx of poor people. Since there was no parking around the cafe, it was difficult for people to come here from the suburbs. Then the phenomenon of the bookstore-coffee houses arose in the suburbs and that drained off a lot of our clientele. It became very difficult to keep the cafe in business. However, the No Exit is currently a coffee house, owned and operated by Michael James and Katy Hogan of the Heartland Cafe. They're booking music there and it's an active place. I hope that it stays around.

Ndikho Xaba performing at the Heartland Cafe, 1995. Photograph by Bob Rugh.

The Howard Street Neighborhood

Boundaries:
Touhy Avenue to Calvary Cemetery (S-N)
Lake Michigan to Clark Street (E-W)

The Howard Street neighborhood in 1900 included two sections: Birchwood Beach and Germania. Both areas were primarily family farms that were intersected by a few main streets, including Clark Street, Sheridan Road and Rogers Avenue (formerly the North Indian Boundary Line). In addition to farmland, trees, scrub brush and sand, there were a few scattered houses throughout the neighborhood. The area between Chase Avenue and Calvary Cemetery in Evanston was considered "no-man's land" because it was outside Chicago city limits. It would not be annexed to the city until 1915. The Birchwood Beach section, the area between Touhy Avenue and Germania, included a small business district near the Chicago, Milwaukee & St. Paul tracks at what became the Jarvis Av-

enue train stop in 1908.

W. P. Brennan, a real estate man in the Howard Street neighborhood remembered what the area was like in the early part of the century. "In 1907 I started my office in the northern part of Rogers Park. There were frame houses on Sheridan Road rather early and the apartments began coming in about 1912 along the road. I remember the speed trap on Sheridan as early as 1910 when it was a boulevard. In 1910, Ben Lowenmeyer subdivided the land from Howard to Calvary and Sheridan to the lake. Before this time it was known as Fisher's Grove and was used for picnics."

Around 1915, with the addition of the final section of the Howard Street neighborhood, Charles W. Ferguson, a real estate developer, built a business block with about a dozen stores and the new Howard Theater. Within a few years, the neighborhood experienced a building boom.

One resident of the Howard Street

neighborhood, broadcaster Norman Ross, has memories of living at 7639 Eastlake Terrace along the lake. "I was born January 30, 1922, in Miami, Florida, and my dad was the world-champion swimmer for the seven years before Johnny Weismuller. When we moved to Rogers Park we lived at the Poinciana Apartment building on Eastlake Terrace, and often in the summertime my dad would swim to Navy Pier from our place, go to work, then swim the ten miles back in the evening. I went to Gale School and wrote a school cheer -- 'One, two, three, four, three, two, one, four, who are we for, Gale, Gale, Stephen F. Gale'."

In the 1930s and 1940s, jazz clubs were very popular on Howard Street and during World War II, men and women from the military would take the elevated, the Chicago and Northwestern Railroad, the North Shore Electric, and buses from the bases at Ft. Sheridan, Great Lakes and Glenview Naval Air Station to visit the bars, restaurants and jazz clubs on

Howard. As a teenager, Joseph Levinson haunted the clubs on Howard. "I graduated from University High on the University of Chicago campus in 1945. The War was ending and I was playing bass with guys who were coming back from the service. I was really into jazz and was playing in a band on campus when I heard about the various jazz clubs around the city, including Howard Street. So, I drove to Howard Street to hear the music at Club Silhouette and Club Detour. I had a great time there."

For Sondra Fargo, a high school student at Evanston Township High School during World War II, Howard Street was where she would go with her friends after school to hang out, eat, dance and listen to the music. "There were lots of hang-out places on Howard Street including White Castle and Howard Bowl. White Castle was just west of the 'El' and was the most popular place to get a quick hamburger. It was open 24 hours a day. As for the jazz clubs, there were the Club Bar-O, Club Silhouette and Club Detour, and there were lots of servicemen in those places. The street was lively and jumping and, as a young person, I could go anywhere without my family being worried where I was or what I was doing.

"I also loved going to the movies at the Howard and Norshore Theaters. Howard Street was the place to go for older kids, including the students at Northwestern University. People today cannot imagine that Evanston was 'dry' and that all the 'blue laws' were in effect everywhere. By the time the War ended in 1945, I couldn't even remember what life

Broadmoor Hotel, Howard and Bosworth, 1927.
(Courtesy of the Chicago Historical Society, ICHi 32278.)

105

Rogers and Clark, looking north, 1925. (Courtesy of the CTA.)

had been like before 1940."

Roger Cooper was born in 1939, and after his parents lived briefly at the Broadmoor Hotel on Howard, they moved to a house at 7625 N. Sheridan Road. "I remember the poultry stores on Howard that sold chickens. You could go in and select them for purchase, and the butcher would slaughter and clean them in the back of the store. In the early to mid-1940s, I remember the ragman who would walk through our alley and sing 'rags for sale.' When I was around seven years old, there was a knife sharpener who would come by, in his 1930's-style truck, and park it in an empty lot behind our building. The neighbors would bring their knives and scissors to him to have them sharpened. The milkman still had a horse-drawn wagon in the early 1940s, and he would deliver milk to our back door."

By the late '40s and early '50s, postwar life in the Howard Street neighborhood was slowly changing, and so was the street. According to Betsy Siegel Sinclair, "Evanston was 'dry' on the north side of the street, but there were bars on the south side. My mother scared me a little because she warned me to be careful when I walked on Howard Street. But, as I remember it, it was a very safe and incredible neighborhood in which to grow up. I used to play baseball in the street on our block (1400 Fargo). It was a big, tree-lined street where kids of all ages would play on the street and sidewalks. When cars would infrequently come down the street, somebody would yell, 'heads up, heads up' and we would all step to the sides of the street before resuming our play."

Linda Lanoff Zimmerman moved to a house in the Howard Street neighborhood at 1515 W. Juneway Terrace in 1946 when she was six years old. "I had begun my education at LeMoyne School in the Lake View neighborhood, but the school didn't have enough books. My parents were not happy with that situation, and they had heard that Gale School was wonderful. So the next thing I knew, we were moving to a big, old house in Rogers Park. I had a great time at Gale, made lots of new friends, and it was only a short walk from my house to school each day."

For Bobbi Rosenthal Cohen, "my early memories of Howard Street are focused on three places -- the Howard Theatre, the Norshore Theatre and the Howard Bowl. We picked the movie theater based on which movie we wanted to see, although the Howard was our favorite. Nearby was Pan Dee's, and when the weather was bad and we couldn't walk home for lunch from Gale School, we would eat there. The other places that I remember on Howard were Mort Gibian's Bootery, the Howard Juvenile Shop, Villa Girgenti's, Papa Milano's, the New Capri, and Oberman's Delicatessen. I would go to Oberman's on Sunday mornings to buy lox and bagels and a newspaper. During the week, since it was close to Gale, we would also stop there for a snack on our way home."

Kiwanis Park, located across from Gale School, was a popular hangout for neighborhood children. Irwin Kanefsky moved to the neighborhood in 1954 when he was eleven years old. "It was a struggle for me because I didn't

Norshore Theater auditorium, c.1930. (Courtesy of the Theatre Historical Society of America.)

Davidson's Bakery on Howard, 1933. Photograph by Hedrich-Blessing.
(Courtesy of the Chicago Historical Society, HB 1846-K.)

know anybody, other than a couple of kids in my building on Birchwood and Ashland. I found my haven at Kiwanis Park and the guy who ran the park, Mack McWilliams, became my athletic mentor. Over the next few years, I spent day and night at that park where we played football, baseball, basketball, and even ice-skated in the winter. It was a great place to stay out of trouble." As for memories of Howard Street, "we would go bowling at Howard Bowl every Saturday, eat sandwiches and ice cream sundaes at Pan Dee's for lunch and spend the afternoon at the Howard Theater."

David Beck grew up in the Howard neighborhood close to Jarvis Avenue, worked behind the counter at Noskin Pharmacy on Jarvis and Greenview, and made deliveries on his bicycle for a Chinese restaurant on Jarvis. "When I was about ten or eleven years old, I had a paper route in the morning that included delivering the *Chicago Sun-Times*, *Chicago Tribune*, *Abenpost*, and the *Daily Forward*. We had to push large carts in the streets and alleys at 5:30 a.m. while freezing our butts off. I stayed with it through Christmas so that I could give my customers a calendar and get their tips." He remembers "Jarvis didn't have much of a beach, so we walked over to Sherwin. We used to love to play on frozen Lake Michigan in winter, and, once, I fell in but I didn't really hurt myself."

Almost all of the students that graduated from Gale went to Sullivan High School. For Betsy Siegel Sinclair, "those were fabulous years. I had many friends from West Rogers Park, but I definitely was an East Rogers Park girl. Sullivan was a 'cool' place, and I loved everything about it. I was in many clubs and ran for office several times. I was a good student and liked all of my teachers. I remember my math teacher, Harry Clare, who used to say, 'Betsy, get your eyes off of Mr. Lindberg's paper. You and your friend, Flora Zee, have reached your mathematical plateau.' I guess that's when I finished taking trigonometry, conceding that I had probably reached my mathematical plateau.

"As to what made Rogers Park so special, I think in the '50s and '60s we were very protected, we got a good education, and we lived in a wonderful neighborhood."

For Linda Lanoff Zimmerman, growing up in Rogers Park "was a positive experience. We were a generation of kids who didn't have to worry about whether or not to do drugs, drink ourselves sick, have sex, or rebel against our parents. It was not our culture in the late 1950s. We did what we thought that we were supposed to do and tried to be as good as we could possibly be in order to make our lives as easy as possible. And, that included not going out with non-Jewish boys."

By the late 1960s and early1970s, the neighborhood demographics began to change and the community began a period of deterioration. Tobey Prinz was one of the leaders in the fight to keep Rogers Park a residential community. She had helped found the Rogers Park Community Council in the 1950s, joined the battle to protect the lakefront from development, focused many of her efforts on the Howard Street neighborhood, and tried to pre-

Touhy Park playground, 1952. (Courtesy of the Chicago Park District.)

Buddy Guy performs at Biddy Mulligans, 1985. Photograph by Marc Pokempner.

vent the deterioration of the community. Tobey worked to create a coalition that became the Rogers Park Committee Against Unemployment and Inflation.

In the 1980s, the Howard neighborhood continued to experience the same racial, ethnic and economic changes that were impacting other parts of Rogers Park and West Ridge. These included an increase in the number of elderly who either moved into retirement homes on Sheridan Road or apartments throughout the neighborhood. Even some former residents had returned to the Howard neighborhood from the suburbs because they liked the idea of raising their families in an integrated community.

The alderman for the 49th ward from 1979 until 1991 was David Orr. He taught at Mundelein College in the early '70s. "I was working for independent Democratic candidates in those years, and often it was an uphill battle, but we were developing as a force in the neighborhood. I think we had the constituency, the demographics and the issues, including an anti-Machine mentality that was fed up with the political corruption. As for issues, there was concern about rental housing and the fact that many senior citizens couldn't afford apartments. In addition, there were bad landlords who caused problems for tenants and weren't maintaining their buildings properly. Our kind of progressive coalition worked on those things, while the more traditional politicians didn't, and that had a lot to do with why we ultimately won the elections."

Shelly Raffel has taught at Gale School

since 1985 and feels that the Howard neighborhood has experienced changes in the past sixteen years. "When I started at the school the demographics were 70% African-American and 30% Hispanic. The numbers have changed. There are now less than 10% Hispanic and the remainder are African-American. The number of students at Gale has declined and not every classroom is filled. I notice that condominiums are being built in the neighborhood for $250,000, but I'm not sure who is buying them. Changes are taking place, but I don't know what the final result will be."

As David Orr has noted, " the Howard Street neighborhood, like other neighborhoods in Rogers Park and West Ridge, includes residents from a wide variety of racial, religious and ethnic groups. The two community areas are probably among the most diverse and most integrated in Chicago, if not the nation."

Mayor Richard M. Daley, Bill Murray and Alderman Joe Moore at groundbreaking for Nathalie Salmon House, 1993.

Police guarding disputed Chicago, Milwaukee, & St. Paul railroad tracks, 1907. (Courtesy of the Chicago Historical Society DN-0005426.)

Charles W. Ferguson, interviewed in fall, 1925

Before 1892 the area around what is now Howard Street was practically all wild prairie and woods. Farmers by the name of O'Leary, Bugner, and Keyes owned most of the land. In 1892 the Germania subdivision, which was the name of this area, was divided into lots and sold to settlers who came with the purpose of making homes there. They did not succeed, however, because they could get no city improvements such as sewers, lights, a school and so forth. Most of them had to sell out; some merely abandoned their land. Otto Freund, Gunderson and others picked up a good deal of this land very cheaply, sometimes merely for taxes. The area was really a part of the town of Evanston, and that town would grant no city improvements. One reason was because the council thought the land to be worthless, especially as the lake washed away parts of the shore at times of great storms. Thus, this district remained unsettled and undeveloped, owned mostly by a few men. The northern limits of Rogers Park were at Chase Avenue.

In 1910 I became interested in the district and bought quite a lot of land. The reason I thought the area could be made into something was because it was a center of transportation in a local sense. The Northwestern Elevated had a station at Howard Street and the Chicago streetcars came to Howard at Clark Street. A few people lived here by that time. Then there was agitation on the part of these landowners to get improvements in the district from the town of Evanston, thus inviting settlement that would result in an increase in the value of the land. We asked for a school, sidewalks and sewers. Evanston turned us down flat. To show how we needed improvements I'll tell you about our sewerage system. We used a ditch that was emptied into the lake although that was against the law. Well, we investigated as to whether the Evanston council wouldn't or couldn't give us improvements, and by gosh, we found out they couldn't. When we saw that Evanston could not fix us up, a movement for secession from Evanston and annexation to Chicago was begun. This was in 1912. A committee of ten men was formed to bring the case before the Evanston council. The council would not hear of secession. Then, I had ballots distributed among the citizens of Evanston and asked them to vote on this subject, whether or not they thought the Evanston council had given the Howard Street people a square deal in refusing them both improvements and secession. The people unanimously voted no, they had not given us a square deal. When the Council saw that the people were against them, they removed their objection to the secession of Howard Street District, or Germania, as they called it.

The next problem was to get the city of Chicago's permission for annexation. They first had to have the bill authorizing the annexation passed by the state government. We only succeeded because the chairman of the house was a brother of one of the agitators. His next thing was to get Chicago to annex us. Here we met some opposition also. Most of the city aldermen did not want to admit a "dry territory" as this section was. However, I talked Alderman Tony Cermak, who had tremendous influence in the city council, into looking favorably upon the annexation. Tony passed the word along that he wanted Howard Street admitted into the city. The annexation [vote] took place on February 8, 1915.

Of course, improvements came now; all except light, which has only just lately been installed. Up until this time we got along with lights bought from Evanston. As a result of this the Howard District, through its improvements, has had a marvelously rapid growth. Howard Street and cross streets are built up with business buildings of every kind. The district is booming larger in the only way it can, that is, expanding west.

Norshore Theatre, 1926. (Courtesy of the Chicago Historical Society, ICHi 32306.)

Patrons in lobby, Norshore Theatre, 1926. (Courtesy of the Chicago Sun-Times.)

Joseph Levinson, jazz musician

I heard about all this music that was being played around town in the 1940s, and one of the places that I'd heard about was Howard Street. Now, from Drexel Square on the South Side to Howard Street is a pretty big hike for a high school kid, especially in those days. But my dad was real good about it, and he let me have the car, and I would go down to Howard Street and park the car. But, one thing you have to know about Howard Street, both during and after the War, was that it was jammed with servicemen. It was absolutely packed with servicemen. They had Great Lakes Naval Training Station, Glenview Naval Air Base, and Fort Sheridan all within a train ride of Howard Street. And Howard Street was to the north side of Chicago what Rush Street was to downtown. Okay, it jumped, at least on the south side of the street. Now, remember that I was a kid, maybe sixteen or seventeen years old, so that my understanding of "dens of paradise," and stuff like that was very limited. I knew that hookers were there. Everybody knew that. But, I never saw any, and I was too young to be approached by any and I wouldn't have known what to do if I had been. But I did know that the music was there and the two places that I knew about were the Club Silhouette and the Club Detour.

I would go to the Club Silhouette, even though I wasn't old enough to be there, I would have to sneak in. Maybe they would throw me out and maybe they wouldn't. I remember listening to Herbie Fields and Charlie Ventura at the Silhouette, and the Fields Octet or Septet was a real powerhouse group that was sort of trying to be a bop group. They were trying to get into that kind of thing. Swing music, like the music played by Benny Goodman and Tommy Dorsey, was beginning to be passé among the hip musicians of the time. By the way, I was hep when it was hip to be hep. In those days I was hep, but I was not a hep cat because I didn't have the zoot suits and the big shoulder stuff and the chain, and all that. A lot of the hep cats would wear a beret and let their goatee grow, and try to be like Dizzy Gillespie. And there were a lot of guys who were smoking joints and doing all kinds of stuff with needles, but, thank God, I never got into that.

I also remember seeing Art Tatum in the Club Detour one night. I screwed up my courage and went in there figuring that they were going to throw me out because I was underage, but nobody did. I sat at the bar at the Detour that was one of those kinds of bars with the piano and the little bandstand behind the bartender. It was like a round bar surrounding the platform where the band was, and there was Tatum, up on the platform all by himself, on a grand piano, in the middle of this bar. He was playing the piano, and hardly anyone was in the club. Either nobody knew he was there, or they hadn't advertised his appearance. So, I sat there, completely blown away, because, by that time, he was like a God to me. He was the greatest jazz piano player that I'd ever heard until then, and he was so advanced that it was scary. There was his technique and his ideas and his harmonics and everything. It was like a graduate school course in how to be totally great on your musical instrument.

Boyd Kelly and band at Club Silhouette, c.1940. Photograph by Henry Green. (Courtesy of the Chicago Historical Society, ICHi 25580.)

Club Silhouette, c.1940. Photograph by Henry Green.
(Courtesy of the Chicago Historical Society, ICHi 32267.)

Casa Bonita, c.1940. Photograph by Henry Green.
(Courtesy of the Chicago Historical Society, ICHi 32257.)

Party at Casa Bonita, 1615 W. Howard, 1946. Photograph by Henry Green. (Courtesy of the Chicago Historical Society, ICHi 25622.)

Larry Lester and his orchestra with Kay Dare, Club Detour, c.1940. Photograph by Henry Green. (Courtesy of the Chicago Historical Society, ICHi 25573.)

June E. Hill, in Letters To The Editor, *Howard News*, **Thursday, August 22, 1935**

I want to 'throw' my opinion in with those of the Howard Business Men concerning the many taverns both on Howard and in Rogers Park in general. Mind you, I am not one of the so-called 'Old Fogies' but belong to the younger generation. As I first remember Howard Street there were a few scattered stores and the Howard Theater. Now as I see it, there are nothing but taverns, which are far from being a moral asset to any neighborhood. Young women cannot walk down Howard Street of an evening because of adventurous drunks who fast become a menace and an annoyance. I am not one condemning men only. Such a condition breeds a hangout spot for women who have not been from conventional society. I have seen such women on Howard Street myself so I am not talking through my hat. It is high time the thriving Rogers Park community got up in arms and rid itself of most of these common and far from comely females so that it would be safe for a respectable citizen to walk down the street without being approached.

Sondra Fargo, editor

In the 1940s, when I was going to Evanston Township High School, we spent a lot of time on Howard Street at the jazz clubs. In those days, everybody danced, and unlike some of the kids who liked to drink, I loved to dance. And, so, except for the Aragon Ballroom on Lawrence Avenue, which was another haunt for all of us, the nearest place was Howard Street. We would go to the little clubs, like The Bar-O and the Club Silhouette, which is where I first saw Sarah Vaughn. All the clubs there had some sort of dance floor, even if they were postage-stamp sized. In fact, I remember that the Club Silhouette was a really nice nightclub. It was located near the 'El', and there were lots of what we always thought of as hangout places. At either The Bar-O or the Club Silhouette was where I saw Billy Eckstine, although nobody knew who he was at that time.

Shecky Greene, comedian

I remember Howard Street because my career really started on Howard at a place called the Club Silhouette. I was going in and out of college at that time, in the 1940s, and the Silhouette had an amateur show. So, I got up and I won the amateur contest. Sarah Vaughn was on the bill at that time, and I'll never forget it because later on, when I became very friendly with Sarah, I told her about that time and she said that she didn't remember it. The Club Silhouette was located east of the 'El' tracks on the south side of Howard. The Bar-O and the Club Detour were near there, but although I knew of their existence, I never really went into those places.

Norm Coughlin, in *The Historian*, Fall 1989

The alleys in the teens and twenties were quite different than they are today. In the main they were muddy and very uneven, but then, so were many streets. After a rain of any consequence, in some areas there was a jumble of large puddles that became quagmires. More than once I saw a large solid-wheeled, chain-driven coal truck have to wait for one of their teams of horses to be hitched to the front bumper and pull them out to dry ground, after they had slid around helplessly. At that time, garbage only was put in galvanized cans for pickup by a team with a heavy metal wagon, a single driver doing all the lifting. In summer, at the height of the melon and sweet corn season, with rinds and cobs added to the other items, an ungodly odor would pervade not only the alley, but sometimes would be gently wafted into many kitchens to complement the heat and humidity. Ashes from the coal-fired furnaces of each home, during the heating season, were put into similar metal containers and bushel baskets to be picked up by a team and a large wooden wagon, with flair boards for overloading. Again, there was a single driver, who really put in a day's work. There was always a cloud of dust hanging over the rig.

Most people hung out the wash in the backyard, so combat-wise housewives learned to change their washdays to a day when the ash wagon did not come through, lest their efforts be in vain. The alleys themselves were reasonably uniform in height, but many yards were quite a bit lower, often causing runoff problems following a rain or a thaw. Also, many neighborhood residents used all available space for flower gardens and vegetable patches, often needed to stretch the food dollar. Some had large lawns graced with a pergola through which roses were entwined with grape vines. Often, a brightly painted stanchion swing would provide hours of amusement for all. Fruit trees, mostly apple or cherry, were squeezed where possible. Most of the wooden Victorian houses had carriage houses, with living quarters opening on to the alleys. Some of these were still in use as such, though autos were steadily coming into style. There were few garages then, and what there were, were for a single car, but some carriage houses had been converted to accommodate cars. Very often, a chicken coop, full of scratching and clucking hens, was built alongside the carriage houses and a pigeon loft generally rose above the coop. Both had apertures in the side of the larger structure so that access was possible in severe weather. Finally, especially if the home's original owners had a European background, there would be a rabbit hutch where the furry habitués would wrinkle their noses and hop about unconcernedly.

Another noteworthy thing from the alley view was that all apartment buildings had open back porches with spindle railings. As time went by, they were "glassed-in" one by one, to provide another room. Still later, those same added rooms were improved further with better windows and siding, inside paneling and heaters. So, the humble old back porch, which once served only as a storage space for a wastebasket and garbage can became useful components of some lovely apartments. Oh yes, porches did serve as hiding places for Christmas trees until Christmas Eve.

Alley bordering the north side of Touhy Park, c.1950. (Courtesy of the Chicago Park District.)

Boys diving into lake at Rogers Avenue Beach, c.1945. Photograph by Henry Green. (Courtesy of the Chicago Historical Society, ICHi 32285.)

Children leaving for YMCA camp, c.1945. Photograph by Henry Green. (Courtesy of the Chicago Historical Society, ICHi 32274.)

Voter registration booth sponsored by Gale School PTA, 1948. Photograph by Henry Green. (Courtesy of the Chicago Historical Society, ICHi 25612.)

Irwin Kanefsky, business owner

I started at Gale School in the mid-'50s when I was eleven years old and in sixth grade. I had moved to Rogers Park from the West Side and it was a little overwhelming because now I was with kids who were really a lot wealthier than I was. I think that school seemed hard because the quality of education was better. In seventh grade, I had a teacher who was a former Marine and who thought that he was still in the Marines. Everything was "yes, sir," and "no, sir." And, if you were a bad kid you went behind the blackboard and he made you stay there. He used to give us three to four hours of homework every night and he said, "I'm preparing you guys for college, and this is the way it is." He ran the class like a barracks.

Linda Lanoff Zimmerman, college educator

When I went to Gale in the '50s I liked to participate in sports. We had jump rope contests and I won the contest, and that was an important thing to me. I used to practice all the time, and Mr. Weiss, the gym teacher, was very supportive and he thought that girls should be athletes at a time when nobody else felt that way. Another memory I have of Gale was that we would always go across the street on Greenview to Hy's, a little store that was owned by Hy and Lil Davidor. Every morning the kids would come in with their pennies and nickels and line up and get penny candies, like the buttons that come on paper, and wax teeth, and those little wax bottles with the sweet, wonderful stuff inside. They also sold school supplies, so if you needed pencils and lined paper, you'd stop at Hy's.

Shelly Raffel, elementary school educator

I have been teaching at Gale School since 1985. It's a rough neighborhood filled with rough kids who I happen to like. So, to me they're not rough, but an outsider would say that they're rough and tough. There are a lot of discipline problems, but the situation hasn't changed and the neighborhood hasn't gentrified in my sixteen years at Gale. I'm sure it has changed to someone who grew up in here in the '50s and '60s, but since I started here, it's always been the same. I teach third grade and I bump into many of the children that I used to know and they're now big, giant boys playing basketball around the school. To me they are still like little boys who say, "Hi, Mrs. Raffel," whenever they see me.

Paulina looking north from Howard, c.1945. (Courtesy of the CTA.)

Joan Wester Anderson, author

I used to go to the Norshore Theatre on Howard Street a lot when I was growing up in the '50s and that became our first chance to meet boys. Even though we went to St. Jerome's, we were kind of segregated, and we played on different playgrounds and couldn't really socialize too much. But, on Saturday afternoons, you could get two movies and cartoons for $.25, and we would get there around one and never leave the theater until five or six. Sometimes you would stay over in the afternoon for the next movie. Of course, we saw the movies, but we were often out in the luxurious sitting area at the Norshore talking to each other in little groups. That also involved deciding who was going to sit with which boy, deciding how far to let them go, which basically was an arm around the shoulder. It was all very innocent and a very "Happy Days" kind of time. The Howard Theatre was just about a block east, but the Howard was just "peanuts" compared to the Norshore because it had a big foyer where you could stand if there ever was a waiting line. The Norshore was just an elegant theater, and although we actually lived closer to the Adelphi on Estes and Clark, the Adelphi was just an ordinary place. Since the Norshore was a Balaban and Katz movie theater like the Granada, it meant that the seats were fabulous and you behaved in there because it was an elegant place.

Linda Lanoff Zimmerman, college educator

When we were in sixth, seventh and eighth grades at Gale, we had this group of boys and girls. We were all like best friends, and every Saturday morning we would go to the Howard Bowl and go bowling. And, then, after bowling, we'd go to Pan-Dee's on Howard Street and we would order greasy hamburgers, fries and ketchup, and Cokes. And that would be our lunch. We would hang out there for a while, and sometimes we'd put the waitress' tip in the glass of water. We were such bratty kids! And, then, after that we would go next door to the Howard Theatre and see Saturday afternoon movies. So, we were gone almost all day. That was our day; that was Saturday.

Mary Jo Behrendt Doyle, historical society executive director

I did most of my shopping on Howard Street. I remember all the stores including the dime store, Woolworth's, on the north side of the street. Then, there were Gene Reid's Bootery on the south side and Mort Gibian's Bootery on the north side of Howard. I used to buy one pair of shoes at one store, and, then the next time I would need shoes, I would go to the other store. There was the Black Cat Shop, which was a card and gift shop, and it was located right west of the Howard Theatre. The little popcorn place was to the east. Then came Gene Reid's and Pan Dee's Restaurant. I went to various dress shops including Kay Campbell's, Loretta Kam, and Della Frocks. I also went to Robert's Card and Gift Shop, which was on Paulina, north of Howard. We also shopped at De's Market, a butcher shop on Paulina, Howard Juvenile, and Davidson's and Heinemann's Bakeries. I bowled at Howard Bowl for many years, and, when I started working at the A. C. Nielsen Company in 1959, I joined their bowling league and bowled there for another thirteen years.

Howard Street, looking east, 1957. Photograph by Merrill Palmer. (Courtesy of the Chicago Sun-Times.)

Howard Street, looking west, 1957. Photograph by Merrill Palmer. (Courtesy of the Chicago Sun-Times.)

David Orr, politician

I think that Rogers Park became a focal point for the counter culture groups of the '70s, '80s and '90s due, in part, to demographics. Historically you see activism where there are universities and where you have people who do not rely upon traditional politics. For example, if you compare Rogers Park at that time with the Far Northwest Side, or another area where there were primarily homeowners and there was a more homogeneous community. They are usually more willing to follow the orders of the political machine. Rogers Park had universities, including Loyola, Mundelein and Northwestern. There were relatively inexpensive apartments available that were located near the lake in a neighborhood that was changing.

A group of us emerged in the late '60s and early '70s that became an organizing group in the neighborhood for the remainder of the twentieth century. I think that it was the constituency, the demographics and the issues of the time. There were the progressive types, the anti-Machine mentality that was fed up with all of the Machine corruption and the issues on housing and senior citizens in Rogers Park where many seniors couldn't afford the housing. In addition, there were bad landlords that caused lots of problems for tenants. You had many seniors who were being priced out with the introduction of condominiums. You had large groups of people who were looking for activism. Our progressive coalition worked on those things, while the more traditional politicians didn't, and that had a lot to do with why we ultimately won the elections.

The economy of the '90s allowed things to happen that had nothing to do with politicians and that couldn't have happened in the '70s or '80s. Now, with this potential economic downturn, I don't know what the future has in store for us. The neighborhood could become heavily gentrified in a few years. It is such an ideal location, and how many places are there where people can live near the lake? We all know that it is a great place, location-wise, and I do think that there have been improvements and I am very pleased. To me it is a special place because of the people and the location. When I say diversity, what I mean is there is a greater level of tolerance for all kinds of people. The amenities are there, but the best thing is the people and what I love about it is the "grass roots." I like people to take charge of their own lives instead of giving up the power to the political party bosses.

I believe in fighting to make the situation better and allowing the people to stand up against the political machine. My vision is that people with less get more and that the economy becomes good enough so that people have jobs and alternatives to work. We need to have alternatives for people. People are people, and we need to focus less on race and superficial economic determinants and more on what they can contribute to the neighborhood.

Alderman Joe Moore protests Rogers Park landlord, 1993. Photograph by Sandy Bertog.

The Ridge Neighborhood

Boundaries:
Peterson Avenue to Howard Street (S-N)
Clark Street to Western Avenue (E-W)

At the beginning of the twentieth century, the Ridge neighborhood included prairie, farmland, small forests of trees, dirt roads and greenhouses throughout the area west of the Ridge, as well as a cluster of houses near the Chicago & Northwestern train station and scattered throughout the neighborhood from east of the Ridge to Clark. There were numerous stores and businesses on Clark, centered between Morse and Greenleaf, as well as the combination police/fire station at Estes.

During the 1900s, there were two well-established institutions in the neighborhood: Angel Guardian Orphanage, built in 1865 near the original St. Henrys Church, which had been constructed in 1851 near Devon and Ridge; and St. Scholastica Academy, opened in 1907, on the west side of Ridge at Fargo.

Angel Guardian Orphanage originally housed one boy and two girls, but slowly grew in population until it required a complex of several buildings, including a grade school, high school, dormitories, and greenhouses. The orphanage operated for over one hundred years until it was closed in the early 1970s. The site was later transformed into the north campus of Misericordia Heart of Mercy, a home for young adults with developmental disabilities. St. Scholastica Academy continues to serve as a Catholic girls' high school for many area students. Until the mid-forties, the Benedictine Sisters of Chicago also operated a grammar school there.

One early twentieth century resident of the Ridge neighborhood, Gladys Van Iderstine Hoagland, came to Rogers Park in 1898 from Toronto, Canada. "My parents bought a house at 6963 N. Hamilton. I remember looking for violets and buttercups in the spring in a swampy area near Pratt and Western. There were bulrushes, frogs and snakes around there and in 1908 Western and Lunt Avenue were not paved. There were deep sand dunes on Ridge and we would dig into them, try to put boards inside, and make little hideaways where we could play. In winter, we would go tobogganing on Lunt and we tried to push them hard enough so that we could get our toboggan as far as Damen Avenue. There were very few cars, and most vehicles were horse-drawn at that time."

John Staerk remembered the Ridge neighborhood in the 1910s. "My father, Karl, was a blacksmith and he used to shoe horses at his shop at 7118 N. Clark Street. He would bring the horses down Ravenswood, which was unpaved at that time, for shoeing. I remember a bad snowstorm in December 1919. Nothing was open and my father wouldn't take his horses out in it because they might break their legs. But, milk had to be delivered and a lot of horses were destroyed because they were taken out in the snow. The West Rogers Park Improvement Association made a snowplow and someone was paid $4 an hour to use his horses to plow the streets and sidewalks."

Sr. Ann Ida Gannon has memories of the area in 1926, when her family lived in a house at 2200 W. Pratt, at Bell. "The block on Pratt to the west of us, and east of Western, was a dirt road with no buildings. The rest of Pratt was a narrow brick road, without sidewalks, and there were gaslights that a man would come and light every night. Between 1926 and 1932, Pratt was widened and they built sidewalks. Bell was called Pingree, and it was a dirt road that was paved half way south of Farwell because Mr. Molloy had a garage there and he needed to make deliveries. West of Western it was mostly prairie. I remember a greenhouse on Farwell and Bell where we would get geranium cuttings every spring."

In 1927, Sr. Vivian Ivantic came to St. Scholastica as a student. "When I arrived, there were still greenhouses in the neighborhood. There had been an oak forest and some cherry trees on the land around the school and to the west toward Western. At one time, the school owned the land from Ridge to Western, but around 1924, they sold the land from Oakley to Western and bought another piece of land south on Ridge. The area around the school was filling up with apartment buildings in the 1920s, but when the Depression began in 1929, building construction halted for the next ten to fifteen years."

Ruth Levin Dauber moved to the southwestern portion of the Ridge neighborhood with her family in 1929 and lived at 6146 N. Oakley, two blocks east of Western and two blocks north of Peterson. "We lived across from the newer section of Rosehill Cemetery, and at that time the neighborhood was built up and included numerous two- and three-flats. There were only a few

Walter R. McCann Newsstand, Greenleaf and Ravenswood, c.1900.

K. Staerk Horse Shoer, 7118 N. Clark, 1925.

Jewish families in the neighborhood. I attended Stone Elementary School, and then went to Senn High School on Ridge and Clark."

The Depression impacted families in different ways. "When it hit in the 1930s, we were not affected as severely as many other people because my father was a pediatrician with many patients. However, my maternal grandfather owned real estate and he lost a lot of property. I recall that there were only a few stores and mostly prairie to the west of Western."

The onset of World War II changed the lives of everyone in the neighborhood. There was a clear sense of fear and foreboding and the families often struggled to save enough ration stamps to purchase daily necessities. There were air raid drills and residents would hang black curtains on their windows to block the light. Jim Kirkpatrick recalls that "during the War, we lived at 1952 W. Morse in the lower level of an old farmhouse. We had an oil space heater, and I remember we got ration stamps to purchase the oil. My mother worried about having enough ration stamps to keep the place heated."

Shopping in the Ridge neighborhood was limited to stores on Clark, Devon and Howard, as well as small commercial centers at Lunt and Western and Touhy and Ridge. Sr. Ann Ida Gannon remembers, "When I was very young, our Christmas shopping was done at a dime store in another neighborhood, so when Woolworth opened a store in our neighborhood, on Clark Street, it was wonderful."

Joan Wester Anderson remembers businesses on Clark including Walgreen's, the First Commercial Bank, Holden's, Green's, Bode's Food Shop, Davidson's Bakery, Fulton's, the Certified Grocers, and Woolworth. "I worked at Woolworth and it seemed that everyone I knew had a job there at one time or another. They would hire 14-year-old kids, and one of the first places they would put us was behind the thread counter."

The Adelphi Theatre at Estes and Clark was a popular movie house for neighborhood residents. Edward Mogul remembers going there in the late '40s and early '50s before television became popular. "I went to the Adelphi with my neighbors on a regular basis, usually arriving early on Saturday morning. We would spend hours there watching thirty cartoons in a row and then *Flash Gordon* and *Superman* and we would come out of the theater with our eyes crossed. Our parents usually gave us just enough money for admission, popcorn and candy."

The business district around Touhy and Ridge included a small group of stores. Mary Jo Behrendt Doyle remembers "Wietor's Drugstore on the corner of Touhy and Ridge. My grandmother used to take me there all the time. There was a row of stores on Touhy, west of Ridge, that were built in the 1950s that included Ernie's Florist, a laundromat, Carlson's Delicatessen and Wirth's Bakery. When I was fourteen, I worked at Harriet's Card and Gift Shop, the last store before the alley. On the east side of Ridge, I recall Grocerland, owned by the Tarrant brothers, a laundry, candy store, and beauty shop."

Steve Chernof also has memories of Carlson's Delicatessen where he "would go and buy sliced roast beef and a container of potato salad. I clearly remember how it tasted because it was so good. And, down the street, where Touhy

merges with Rogers Avenue, was the barbershop. I can still picture the barber."

Some neighborhood residents shopped near Lunt and Western. Cameron Dall has memories of "Glow Drugs, where we used to get prescriptions filled and buy candy. Mr. Glow looked like a typical pharmacist because he always wore a white jacket. Across the street was Baskin-Robbins 31 Flavors Ice Cream. Next door was a barbershop where I used to get haircuts. There was the

Quality Grocery Market owned by Mr. Kammisch, who always wore a straw hat and apron. It was an old store with wooden floors and a butcher shop in the back. The butcher would give us a piece of sausage as a treat. On our birthdays, we were allowed to select a little stuffed animal as a gift from the rack of toys in the front of the store." Dale Lichtenstein has memories of two stores located at Farwell and Western, "Hershenson's Drugstore had a soda fountain and Napshin's Quality Foods was

Laying of cornerstone for new building, May 19, 1929, Angel Guardian Orphanage. (Courtesy of the Archdiocese of Chicago, Joseph Cardinal Bernardin Archives and Records Center.)

Children's garden club, Pottawattomie Park, c.1945. (Courtesy of the Chicago Park District.)

owned by Dave Napshin who lived in the back of the store."

Jerry Wester remembers the hill at Lunt and Ridge. "The 'hill' was the place to be in the 1950s, and I had a Radio Flyer. I used to spend all summer pulling that red wagon to the top of the hill and then coasting back down. My dad helped me build boxcars and my friends and I would race them down Morse from Ridge. The faster you could get them going, the bigger hero you were to your friends. Kids also put baseball cards in the spokes of their Schwinn bicycles so that they would sound like they had motors."

There were a couple of parks in the neighborhood where the children could play: Pottawattomie Park, on Rogers Avenue west of the Chicago & Northwestern Railroad tracks; and Paschen Park, on Lunt at Damen. Don Pardieck remembers Paschen Park. "It was called Lunt Park in the '50s, and they used to freeze it in the wintertime for ice-skating. In the late '50s they installed lights in the park and we used to play softball there at night. It was a little park, with a gravel surface. During softball games, the older kids could easily hit the roof of the field house when they batted. The roof was made of shingles that would often break off as the softballs came bouncing down."

Mary Jo Behrendt Doyle has fond memories of Pottawattomie Park. "We spent many enjoyable hours there after grammar school at St. Margaret Mary's. I fondly remember Ms. Boldineau who taught arts and crafts at the field house."

Children in the Ridge neighborhood went to grammar school at St. Scholastica, St. Margaret Mary, St. Henrys, Stone School, Armstrong School, or Bartleme School, which was open for several years on Ridge, south of Pratt, to handle some of the overcrowding at Armstrong.

"I went to Armstrong in the 1950s," remembers Andy Halpern, "and although the student population there was diverse, a majority of the kids were Jewish. My fourth grade teacher was Ms. Bates and her classroom was particularly interesting because it was filled with pictures of different species of birds. I clearly remember Mrs. Minogue, the principal. She was a lovely white-haired lady whom the kids liked."

Barbara Cherney Mackevich began at Armstrong in the seventh grade. "I was able to quickly make new friends. I remember Ms. Raditz, the gym teacher, who taught us the 'Armstrong Waltz' and square dancing. Ms. Mulholland was the home economics teacher and among other skills we learned in her class was how to open a variety of locks that had been placed on a wooden board." Betty Serlin Covici had the impression that Armstrong "was a really strict school. Social events didn't seem to be a priority there. There wasn't a lunch program in the '50s and I walked home several blocks to have lunch at our apartment every day. I remember having to do a lot of walking to visit with friends. It seemed that nobody lived near each other."

Angel Guardian Orphanage was home for many orphans during its more than one hundred-year existence, providing education, housing, training in the trades, and religious education. Students from the orphanage also participated on sports teams and competed against private schools in baseball, basketball and football. Rick Kogan recalls playing football against a team from Angel Guard-

A.C. Nielsen Company, 2101 W. Howard, 1945. Photograph by Hedrich-Blessing. (Courtesy of the Chicago Historical Society, HB-08235-S.)

St. Margaret Mary School, 2324 W. Chase, 1951.

ian in the 1960s. "I played for the Latin School and Angel Guardian was one of our opponents. When my father, Herman Kogan, was growing up in Humboldt Park in the 1920s and 1930s, he used to play tennis at the courts at Angel Guardian. The tennis courts were among the only ones in the city available to the public. It was fascinating to me that he would take two or three buses just to get to those courts."

From 1965 to 1974, Marcee McGinnis Williams attended Stone School at Granville and Leavitt. "I was blessed with a wonderful group of teachers at Stone. Principal Celia Rosensweig ran the school with an iron fist and we both feared and respected the woman we called 'Rosie.' I made a number of life-long friends at Stone and we reminisce about our days there when we get together."

By the late 1960s, the Ridge neighborhood began to experience social and demographic changes. Those shifts were reflected at Sullivan High School, which many neighborhood teens attended. Dale Lichtenstein recalls "during the time I went to Sullivan, from 1967 to 1971, the school's population started to change. By the mid-1970s, the Jewish population at the school had been dramatically reduced to less than 50% from a previous high of almost 90%. The school building was quite gloomy, and during the Vietnam War years there was a lot of drug and alcohol use by the students. Our social life was pretty wild during the so-called 'sexual revolution'."

The Ridge neighborhood continued to change by the time Marcia Froelke Coburn bought a 100-year-old house on Greenleaf, east of Ridge "When we moved here in April 1976, the neighborhood was filled with big houses that were primarily owned by German and Irish Catholic families with lots of kids. However, within a few years, people began to move away as their children grew up. The houses were too big for them, and the neighborhood seemed less safe. In the 1980s, there was an increase in subsidized housing and a number of halfway houses opened nearby. Some neighborhood residents panicked and left. However, by the '90s, people realized that the houses were a great value and started to move back. I feel really good about the neighborhood today, and I think that more professionals will continue to buy property here."

Tim Cavey was born in the Ridge neighborhood in 1981, and he and his family lived in a house at Touhy and Damen. "My great-grandfather built the house in 1916. When I grew up there, I played baseball at Pottawattomie Park, shopped on Clark Street, and attended grammar school at St. Margaret Mary's. I didn't have any nuns as teachers there, but we had religion class every morning. Although the neighborhood went through changes and new groups of people moved in, the diversity is one of the things that I liked about living in Rogers Park. My memories of living in the Ridge neighborhood are really wonderful. I can't imagine how it would have been growing up anywhere else."

Child on swing, Ravenswood and Greenleaf, 1990.

Gladys Van Iderstine and friends, 6900 block of Hamilton, c.1915.

Joseph Winkin, interviewed in February 1928

I came from the old country in 1870 and coming up here on the Ridge, I worked for the farmers around here. When I bought my own farm where I live now on Ridge Boulevard there was nothing but sand from Ridge east to the North-western tracks. But I grew things all right on it. So did the other people along the Ridge. It was all farms south of Howard Street until William Mason subdivided. He started out twelve years ago and the street end sewers were put in. But the biggest building in the district has been in these last three years. The only thing I can tell you about the annexation to Chicago is that some of us farmers did not want it. We had large acre property then and we knew that the increase in taxes would be a lot for those times. Being in Chicago didn't increase our income any, either. The taxes were higher the next year after we went in and it went so hard on some of the farmers that they were ruined completely. Yes, sir, it would have been just as good if we never went into Chicago.

Jack Marshall, interviewed in February 1928

The stores didn't come into West Ridge before 1890. Before that time there had just been a few south of Greenleaf on Ridge. Trausch had a grocery and a saloon next to it just north of the priest's house at Ridge and Devon on the west side of the street. There weren't more than four hundred people in this whole district from Howard to Devon and Clark to the north branch in 1900 so there was no need of stores. We went to Clark Street for everything, or up to Evanston. Then the grocery stores and meat markets peddled food in those times. Besides, everyone had a team of horses and drove into town when they wanted things. We used to drive to Chicago more than you would think. It took three to five hours though. There was a shoe store that kept open on Sunday so that the people coming to church could get shoes. This was near St. Henry's on Ridge where the shoe shop is now. Joe Ebert had a restaurant on Ridge across from the Standard Oil station. This was later called Ebert's Grove.

Azile Reynolds, interviewed in February 1928

The large supply of greenhouses west of us [Armstrong School] make this spot fly-stricken in the fall and they are so thick that you can't read a book in front of you. The Board of Education provided screens for the office windows, but there is a law against screen doors in exit doors, so the flies come in here and stay because they can't get out.

Boy's playground, Angel Guardian Orphanage, 1917. (Courtesy of the Archdiocese of Chicago, Joseph Cardinal Bernardin Archives and Records Center.)

Patriotic scene, Angel Guardian Orphanage, 1918. (Courtesy of the Archdiocese of Chicago, Joseph Cardinal Bernardin Archives and Records Center.)

May Festival, St. Scholastica Academy, c.1920.

146

May Festival, St. Scholastica Academy, c.1920.

Baseball game, Angel Guardian Orphanage, c.1930. (Courtesy of the Archdiocese of Chicago, Joseph Cardinal Bernardin Archives and Records Center.)

Shop class, Angel Guardian Orphanage, c.1940. (Courtesy of the Archdiocese of Chicago, Joseph Cardinal Bernardin Archives and Records Center.)

Kids opening Christmas presents, Angel Guardian Orphanage, c.1940. Photograph by Henry Green. (Courtesy of the Chicago Historical Society, ICHi 32287.)

Ray Thill, mechanical engineer

I came to Angel Guardian around 1946, when I was ten years old, and I was there with my two brothers and three sisters. I'm the oldest of the six of us, and I lived at Angel Guardian for about six years until I got out of high school. I didn't have too much of a choice about being there because my father had died and my mother couldn't support six kids by herself. It wasn't my preferred location, but, in retrospect, I probably turned out better by being there than if I had bummed around with the people I was growing up with at the time.

As for the school, I was in sixth grade when I first lived there and the classes were small because of the nature of the place. The nuns were strict because they had to keep people on their toes, and we could use a little bit of that kind of discipline in this day and age, especially the way kids are raised today. I was involved in a variety of sports at Angel Guardian, including football and basketball. After I left there, the Orphanage bought up some more land near Granville and built a baseball diamond. There weren't more than twenty-five kids in each high school class. The activities for the kids in high school were limited to the grounds of the orphanage, except by special permission, or we were supervised on trips around the neighborhood. During high school years, we worked half a day in one of the trades in order to help maintain the property. I was a painter and I painted anything that didn't move. There were about four of us in that particular group, and there were carpentry and print shop and automobile mechanics classes. Angel Guardian had probably just about anything that kids needed to learn a trade. I used to earn some extra spending money on Saturdays by doing work for people in the neighborhood who wanted their houses painted. Of course, they couldn't beat the low prices that we were charging them, and we were getting a little extra spending money.

There were boys and girls in classes together, although they weren't housed together in the dormitories. In grammar school, there were thirty-four kids in a cottage and that meant there were a lot of beds in a large room, along with lockers and places to wash. As for showers, they were down the street and across the way, and everybody showered once a week in a mass shower. The nuns supervised you all the time you were away from your dormitory. In high school, all of the freshmen and sophomores were in one dorm, the juniors and seniors were in another dorm and there were about 100-150 kids in the high school. As for social events, they had dances, but considering the nature of Angel Guardian, the social aspect wasn't something that got a high priority. It wasn't a real conducive atmosphere for dating. I saw the other kids all the time, and in high school we started classes at 6:30 a.m. until late in the afternoon. We also had night school every night and that kept us busy in the evening. There wasn't any television at the time so occasionally we would listen to the radio. I got out of Angel Guardian in 1954, graduated from Illinois Institute of Technology [IIT] in 1958, and became a mechanical engineer. As I look back on the experience, I understand the circumstances that brought me to Angel Guardian and I don't blame my mother for us being there. She visited us regularly at the orphanage, and, in fact, my mother had been raised there when she was younger.

Dance performance, St. Scholastica Academy, c.1925.

May Crowning, St. Scholastica Academy, c.1930.

Picture day, St. Scholastica Academy, 1944.

Joan Wester Anderson, author

The typical legend at St. Scholastica during the '50s was that as the new freshmen came in, the older girls would tell them that there was a swimming pool on the fourth floor, and that to pass initiation they were supposed to go up there and jump in the pool. Well, the fourth floor of the school was actually part of the convent. It wasn't closed, and if you lost count of how many floors that you had run up, you could easily run up that last set of stairs and be right in the convent with the nuns running around with no headdresses on. Every year there was always some innocent freshman who would go up to the fourth floor to see the pool. Of course we didn't have a pool, and never had a pool. So, that was how you got initiated to Scholastica.

We also had an event every year when each member of the senior class adopted a freshman and they did a lot of activities together. I think that was always part of what made Scholastica such a warm place. There was always someone there that a new person had a name for, could eat lunch with and do other things with during those first few months at the school. That way, new students could ease into the school routine and not feel that they were there all by themselves. The student body was drawn from all over the surrounding suburbs. Students who lived near to Scholastica on Ridge would walk to school, but a lot of girls took buses. We called ourselves the St. Scholastica "Susies," and each class had its own song, too. So, when we were at an assembly and it was finished, each class would sing its song and it meant that part of moving from freshman up to senior was that you would sing the next year's song. Many of my friends have talked over the years about what it was about St. Scholastica and its students that made the girls and the school so different from other Catholic girls' high schools. I think it was that St. Scholastica really cherished the individual student.

There was one very serious offense at St. Scholastica. No one could smoke in the bathrooms or in the Circle driveway in front of the school. If you were caught smoking in the Circle, you would be expelled and almost no one ever smoked there because they knew that the nuns would never give them a second chance on anything when they said they wouldn't. And I remember that in my junior year, there were two seniors who were caught smoking in the Circle and they were expelled. So, the nuns meant business. There was a great deal of attention paid to achievement, but it wasn't all grades. The nuns wanted to develop the whole woman and they always believed that we could do anything. That was long before the Feminist Movement ever happened. In May of each year, there was always a May Crowning. We just walked outside in a procession and you would say the rosary and then one person would crown the Blessed Mother, because May was considered her month. All the parishes had a May Crowning, and the crown was just made out of flowers and one of the songs we sang was *"Bring Flowers of the Rarest, Bring Flowers of the Fairest."*

Story hour at Pottawattomie Park, c.1945. Photograph by Henry Green. (Courtesy of the Chicago Historical Society, ICHi 25616.)

Dress party, 2110 W. Birchwood, c.1945. Photograph by Henry Green. (Courtesy of the Chicago Historical Society, ICHi 32276.)

Winners of Parade on Wheels contest, Pottawattomie Park, c.1945. Photograph by Henry Green. (Courtesy of the Chicago Historical Society, ICHi 25617.)

Sr. Ann Ida Gannon, college administrator

My first year of teaching high school was 1941, the year of Pearl Harbor. I can still remember the effect of that on the families I was teaching. Many of the young women had to deal with their brothers going off to the War. There was rationing, and we Sisters didn't need much. We were wearing habits, so we had extra coupons for shoes and clothes that we often would give to the students. I was aware of various foods that were being rationed, including coffee. As much as we could, we tried to share with the families. We didn't have television in those days, and, at times, the news was long in coming even though there was radio. But my chief recollection is the effect that the War had on the families.

Jim Kirkpatrick, computer consultant

I was a young kid during World War II and I remember feeling afraid of what was happening. I also remember talking with my friends at Armstrong School about the Germans. As kids, we used to play our own "war games" and hunt the Nazis in the school playground. The real concern of my mother was that she would have enough ration stamps for food, and for enough oil to keep our home heated.

Ray Thill, mechanical engineer

When I was younger, before I was at Angel Guardian, we lived in the neighborhood around Pottawattomie Park. They used to have paper collecting contests during WW II where kids used to go out in the neighborhood to collect papers and they would give the winner two tickets to a Cubs game. I came close once to winning the contest. We used the park facilities to go to arts and crafts classes, and I learned how to make potholders and tried to sell them to make extra money. One of the things that is very vivid in my mind, is when the War ended in 1945 we had amassed a big stack of newspapers. We lived on Honore, near Rogers Avenue, along the railway tracks, and my friends and I decided to tear up all the papers and make confetti. We walked around the neighborhood and threw the torn up newspapers all over the place. It seemed like a good thing from a sixth grader's viewpoint as a way to celebrate the end of the War, but the neighbors got mad because they didn't want to clean up the mess that we had made.

Azile Reynolds, interviewed in February 1928

I came to Armstrong School as the principal in 1912 when it was opened. At that time the school was located in a grove of oak trees with a great deal of brush and weeds. The oak trees were a distinguishing feature and the place was called Oak Grove before the school was built. The people in Rogers Park used it for a picnic grove. This site was chosen for the school because of the high location of the ground just west of Ridge Boulevard. A site in the southeastern part of the district east of Ridge and north of Devon had been considered, but the land was too low and the site was too close to the older section of Rogers Park. It was thought better to put the school west of the Ridge since the population in West Ridge had to grow west. In 1912, there were three houses north of us on Touhy, two on Greenleaf and none on Pingree (later Bell Avenue). In fact, there was very little to the west of us. It has just been recently that the district around Western and west of it has grown up. Five years ago the streets were paved over west, but most of the houses have come in since 1925.

Jim Kirkpatrick, computer consultant

I went to Armstrong School in the 1940s, and I remember the fabulous steam engines that were in a hallway just below the first floor. I was interested in mechanical things and was fascinated with the high-pressured boilers. I used to talk to the school engineer about those machines. As for special events at the school, we had an annual fair with a book sale and races and other athletic events. One memory about Armstrong that I have is that someone would go around the room with a quart-sized jar of ink and fill up the glass inkwells on the desks.

Dale Lichtenstein, sales manager

I remember going to Armstrong School in the 1960s. My kindergarten teacher, Mrs. Kidd, was just terrific. In those days, they still served milk in glass bottles and we had to shake them up because the cream was settled at the top. The playground was covered in sand and I remember that every June they would have Field Day. It was a big festival with races, rides and food. It was wonderful and a great way to build community spirit. Kids would come with their parents. At Christmas time, we used to put on plays as part of a big Christmas pageant. We would spend almost three weeks practicing for it and whole school would be involved. Everyone would get dressed up in costumes and we'd march and sing songs. It was just a wonderful time.

Gena Martinez Zalenka, librarian

I remember our yearly Christmas play. All the grades at Armstrong were involved in that event. I was in various plays and as a kindergartener I was a teddy bear and we danced around the stage. In fifth grade, I played an Irish washerwoman and did a tap dance. In seventh and eighth grades we were in a procession and carried homemade lanterns made out of oatmeal boxes with different color paper and a flashlight shone through them. We always shoved candy in our lanterns because we had to sit there for two hours on the Assembly Hall stage while everyone performed. We were in a processional singing *God of Our Fathers* and *Angels We Have Heard on High*. Because there was a heavy Jewish population at Armstrong, we also danced the horah and sang Chanukah songs.

Students, teachers, and Tess the dog at Armstrong School, 1992.

Betty Major Rose, interviewed in July 1994

I was born in New Orleans in 1946 and lived there until I was ten years old before we moved to Oakland, California. We moved back to New Orleans several years later and then, in April 1971, I came up to Chicago for a visit. I saw a snowfall and because it was so beautiful and there were distinctive seasons, I decided to move here. So, I went back to New Orleans, packed up the kids and moved to the Lincoln Park neighborhood. However, after my daughter, Ginneria, was killed in Chicago as a result of gang violence, I moved back to New Orleans for five months because I was trying to run away and forget the terrible thing that happened. But I know now, and I knew after I had moved, that you really cannot run away from your pain and you have to deal with it. I decided to come back to help others in similar situations to deal with the kind of emotions I had experienced.

As a result of Ginneria's death, my husband and I formed Parents Against Gangs and we do a lot of hospital and advocacy work and grief counseling. We have a program that we operate out of Illinois Masonic Hospital and have tried to get the counseling program established at all the trauma centers within Chicago, and hopefully, around the country. It has been untiring work and I could do it all the time. We do a lot of seminars and workshops and speak to schools, churches, and community groups about gang prevention. I work at a suburban Cook County courthouse and focus on enforcing the drug nuisance laws and trying to reduce the use and sales of drugs. I work with many law enforcement agencies, community organizations and churches as well as helping to enable landlords and building managers to evict any individual who is selling or using drugs.

I moved to Rogers Park in 1985, and we lived on the 7400 block of Winchester. It was a tree-lined street in a quiet neighborhood. Even though Rogers Park is not as quiet as it was in 1985, that particular strech, from Rogers Avenue to Howard Street, is really still the same as it was when I first came to the neighborhood. A nice thing about my block is that the neighbors know each other, and every Christmas my neighbor bakes fruitcake for all of the neighbors. We all watch out for each other.

Rogers Park has a gang problem and I think that people have begun to acknowledge that and the need to have community centers for the kids. There are many factions in Rogers Park, but I think that if we all come together and not remain so divided then we can do a better job of dealing with gangs and drugs. A youth center would be a neutral ground and a safe haven. It would provide the kids with something that is recreational and educational for their free time. The kids have so much energy that a youth center would get them to focus on more positive things. But, so far, people haven't been able to agree on how to meet the need.

One of my other concerns is that I don't see enough African-American churches in Rogers Park. We need more of those types of religious institutions in the neighborhood because the church is a strong foundation and an important base for the community. African-Americans are very religious and we get so much comfort from our churches.

Betty Major Rose and family with quilt made in memory of her daughter Ginneria, 1983. Photograph by Phil Moloitis.

The West Rogers Park Neighborhood

Boundaries:
Devon Avenue to Howard Street (S-N)
Western Avenue to Kedzie Avenue (E-W)

At the turn of the twentieth century, the West Rogers Park neighborhood was characterized by prairie, farmland, stands of trees and bushes, dirt roads, bogs and springs, scattered farmhouses, greenhouses and few businesses and stores.

Clarence Hess remembers that his grandparents came to the neighborhood in the 1880s and bought the land that would later become Indian Boundary Park. They built greenhouses around Estes, west of Western. "After my parents were married in 1915, they worked in the greenhouses with my grandparents. In 1916, grandfather was the first to get cucumbers and tomatoes to market for Christmas. He sold them in Chicago for $14 a box and got $11,500 payment for the crop."

The major industry was the brick factory at the western edge of the West Rogers Park neighborhood. A large tract of land south of Touhy and west of California was sold to the National Brick Company in 1905, and in 1909 the construction of the Metropolitan Sanitary District Canal provided the clay that would be used in making the bricks. Many Germans and Scandinavians came to West Rogers Park to find jobs, and, between 1912 and 1915, many worked on a housing subdivision that was begun near the brickyards, canal and clay pit. For early residents, life in West Rogers Park was similar to that of a small, rural town, with farms and greenhouses still dominating the neighborhood.

According to Alan Gruenwald, born in 1920, "I remember the brick factory very well. I was chased away from there many times when we were playing in the clay pit. As late as 1934 I shot ducks and geese with my bow and arrow in the clay pits. The brick factory was between Kedzie and the canal, and they had contracts with Chicago to make bricks that were used as paving blocks for streets and buildings in the city."

By 1930, the section of the neighborhood between Western and California had reached residential maturity that included single-family homes, duplexes and apartments, as well as a group of stores around Lunt and Western, near Indian Boundary Park. But most of the area west of California did not experience a building boom until after World War II.

Nancy Bild Wolf's family moved into their new house at 2941 W. Fitch in 1930. "My mother chose the location because she wanted to bring her children to the country, and, at the same time, she didn't like the idea of living in an area with just one ethnic group. She felt that it would be a good experience to live with people from other cultures and religions. I think that we were among the first Jewish families to live in that part of West Rogers Park where there were Luxembourgers, many Greeks, and mostly Catholics."

Her brother, Sidney Bild, remembers their yellow brick, octagonal bungalow, and the surrounding neighborhood of houses, empty lots, and the clay pit west of the dirt road that became Sacramento Avenue. "The clay pit was a great resource for the West Rogers Park community. It ran from North Shore to Touhy, and it had two areas of depth that ranged from a gentle slope to a drop of almost thirty feet. The drop was so deep that it was void of vegetation. It looked quite stark and I thought of it as the 'bowels of hell'." As for the undeveloped nature of the neighborhood, Sidney remembers "that there were a number of truck farms along Touhy from Washtenaw to McCormick where people lived on a few acres of land and grew vegetables which they sold from little stands that they had erected on Touhy."

Howard Fink and his family moved to the area in 1940 and lived in a new house at 2948 W. Estes. He remembers playing in the empty lots and the clay pit, shopping with his mother at the few stores at Lunt and California, and going to the hot dog stand at the northeast corner of Touhy and California. "Every spring, Paul would drive up in an old 1930s car that he used to tow a hot dog stand and would set up 'Paul's Umbrella.' We knew when he was going to be there, and, sure enough, he and his wife would arrive and sell those great hot dogs with celery salt all summer. He was bringing the city to those of us who lived in the country and his arrival was a way of measuring the seasons."

Fink attended Rogers School and then Senn High School. "I was raised in an area of West Rogers Park in the '40s and '50s where going to Senn was very important to us. At that time, it was very good academically and it happened to have fine athletic teams. All I ever thought about before I got to Senn was playing in a Senn-Sullivan football game, and it actually happened. As far as the social structure was concerned, Senn had very definite lines drawn and

Mary and Julia Turner property, between Pratt and Touhy at Kedzie, 1908. (Courtesy of the Metropolitan Water Reclamation District.)

165

Wiltgen Farm, Fargo and California, c. 1910.

people didn't seem to break through those lines until their senior year."

Burt Sherman moved into his new house at 2733 W. Sherwin in December 1941. "The house was built by Mr. Jackson, and he had designed it in a fashion that was unique for its time. We had no windows that faced north, but the house had a big terrace window/door combination that was the width of the living room and it opened up onto a patio looking south. There were two small windows in the front of the room and the house looked like a fort. When we moved in, ours was only the third house on the block, and the other two houses had been built in the early '30s. Across the street from us was an empty lot which we used as our private football field."

Gary Berg remembers that there was a bridle path that ran along the Metropolitan Water Reclamation District Canal. "They called it the 'million dollar bridle path'," and it went from the gas tank at North Shore all the way to Winnetka. There were stables at Touhy and McCormick and my sister used to keep her horse there and ride it on the bridle path. When we first moved to West Rogers Park in the early '40s, there was a big farm on Pratt, just west of California, and the owner was a man whom the kids knew as 'Fatty the Farmer'."

Joseph Epstein moved to 6649 N. Campbell in 1948 at the age of eleven. "West of California and north of North Shore there were newer and grander homes than the one we owned. The area was pretty well developed, and the empty lots in the neighborhood continually filled in with new houses. There were a lot of two-flats and some bungalows. George S. May, the great industrial engineer and owner of the Tam-O-Shanter Country

Indian Boundary Park lagoon, with Park Castles in background, c.1930.

Club, lived in a house on Talman and owned a two-flat that he used for his offices. He also had a limousine and a driver who wore a black suit and hat.

"After first living in the Morse neighborhood and attending Field School, I attended Boone School when we moved to the West Rogers Park neighborhood. After graduation, I went to Senn because I was in that district. At Senn, there were clear divisions among the fraternities and sororities that were Jewish or gentile. As for academics, I was completely disinterested. My friends and I discov-ered more fun in sports and social life at places like Harry's School Store on Glenwood, north of Peterson where I had my first bacon, lettuce and tomato (BLT) sandwich. When we were juniors and seniors, we arranged our schedules so that we could finish classes by noon. Then we would drive to Ashkenaz for lunch and knock down a bowl of kreplach soup and a chocolate phosphate."

Ron Menaker remembers moving to West Rogers Park. "When World War II ended, my father bought a home at 2917 W. Jarvis. It was late 1945

Tennis lessons, Indian Boundary Park, 1946.
(Courtesy of the Chicago Park District.)

or early 1946, and we were among the early Jewish pioneers of our part of the neighborhood. I recall when Mel Thillen's brother, Ferdinand, decided to build a baseball field for the neighborhood kids. He cleaned out the area south of Chase, near Francisco, all the way to Touhy. It had been prairie and farmland, but 'Ferdy' gave us our very own 'Field of Dreams.' That field became a wonderful place to play ball."

Menaker also has strong memories of Rogers School in the early '50s. "The school building was still its original size when I was going there. There were about eight or nine classrooms but no auditorium or gym. So we would have our gym classes by running up and down the hallway. We had a baseball team in grammar school that played at Rogers Park, which was next to the school. The team was sponsored by Mayor Daley's Youth Foundation, and we would travel around the city to play teams from other parks."

Janie Friedman Isackson moved to 2742 W. Fitch in West Rogers Park from the North Town neighborhood. She had begun school at Clinton, but transferred to Rogers in 1949. "Mr. Eckblatt built our house and he took a personal interest in maintaining the quality of each of his newly constructed houses. I remember soon after we moved there on November 1, 1949, there was a big snowstorm. I went outside and was so excited that we lived in a house of our own that I dropped down in the snow and kept rolling around in it as a way of celebrating. The neighborhood was growing so quickly that Rogers School had to go on shifts. When I went to school on the afternoon shift, I would wake up early in the morning and walk with my friends to Indian Boundary Park where we would play, feed the animals, ride our bikes, and make helicopters out of the catalpa pods that had dropped from the trees."

Michael Zelmar moved to the neighborhood in 1951 and lived at 2920 W. Fitch. "By the time I was thirteen or fourteen, I worked at Cal-Touhy Pharmacy on the southwest corner of Touhy and California. I started as a soda jerk, was promoted to cashier, and by the time I was sixteen years old, I became a delivery driver. Many people went to Cal-Touhy for sodas and sundaes, to use the pharmacy and buy newspapers, candy, cigars and cigarettes. Around the corner were Louie's Noshery Restaurant, Paul's Umbrella and Terry's Red Hots. All the teen-agers would hang out at those places during grammar and high school years."

Joel Weisman remembers moving to West Rogers Park at 3017 W. Fargo in 1954. He spent his early years in Albany Park, but his parents wanted to live in a new neighborhood that was Jewish and had ample public transportation to meet the needs of a one-car family. "It was a booming neighborhood in the '50s. There were lots of houses being built, and my grandfather, who was a barber, knew a farmer who owned a forty-acre farm on Touhy and Francisco. The farmer kept trying to convince my grandfather to buy land there and develop houses

Bates Jewelry Store at the Howard and Western Shopping Center, c. 1959.

Ambulance donation to Israel,
Magen David Adom, 1991.

-- but my grandfather knew how to give haircuts, not build houses. I remember the brickyard and the canal west of us, where we would dare to ice-skate in the winter. We would play in the excavation ditches in the summer and sometimes the kids would fall in and get hurt."

After Weisman graduated from Rogers in the mid-1950s, he attended Sullivan High School. "At Sullivan, I was in a club called the Centaurs. We were maniacs and, as I recall, we thought that school was for having fun, not learning. However, I was involved in many activities at Sullivan including being treasurer of the Student Council and the Key Club and editor of the school paper, the *Sentinel*. I used to have a column called 'Words from a Weisman.' That was probably the beginning of my career in journalism."

Marsha Schwartz Landau came to West Rogers Park when she was eight years old after having lived in Chicago's West Garfield Park neighborhood. " We moved to 3104 W. Sherwin in June 1952 and our house was on a street that dead-ended at the brickyards. It was so unsightly there that the neighbors pitched in and landscaped the end of the block so we wouldn't have to look at the brick factory. The kids on our block played together and I remember that almost everyone was Jewish. In those days, there were children in every house and mothers stayed home to raise the kids."

In 1956, Shari Phillips Kanefsky, remembers moving from Granville and Fairfield to the second floor of a new two-flat across from Indian Boundary Park on Estes near Rockwell. "I went to Field School first and then attended Clinton School, before we moved to the West Rogers Park neighborhood and I transferred to Rogers School. Rogers

was a new, modern school and it was the first time that I had male teachers and a male principal. I remember there were clearly defined cliques at Rogers, and most of the kids seemed to live in rich, middle-class Jewish households in big, fancy houses. But I was accepted into those groups and we hung out around Touhy and California."

Similar to many residents of West Rogers Park, Susan Rosenberg RoAne moved to the neighborhood from Chicago's West Side. "We lived at 6639 N. California, between North Shore and Albion, from the time I was in sixth grade until my freshman year of high school at Mather when we moved to a house at Chase and Sacramento. When I was going to Boone, we would hang out at the Nortown Theater on Saturdays with friends, go shopping on Devon and eat at Randl's or Kofield's. The kids from Boone became friendly with their compatriots from Clinton. When we were ready to graduate from grammar school, a group of us from Boone and Clinton had a meeting at the North Town Library on California because we knew that we were going to have to give up our school identities and meld together at Mather."

Alvin Blackman was a seventh grade teacher at Rogers School from 1959 through 1968. "When I came there in 1959, big changes had already taken place in the neighborhood. West Rogers Park was pretty well saturated with houses, although there had been empty lots around the school only a few years earlier. The population of Rogers had grown from only 380 children in 1951 to almost 1,300 kids with morning and afternoon shifts by that time. Every classroom was used and most teachers had 40-48 children in a classroom. The children were polite and the parents sought out the teachers for counseling and advice. By the '70s and '80s, the role of the teacher changed with the onset of neighborhood councils. Many teachers and principals left the profession when the demands became unreasonable."

Dan Miller moved with his family to West Rogers Park in 1968 when he joined the *Chicago Daily News*. He bought a Chicago-style brick bungalow at 6742 N. Talman, a half-block south of Pratt. "Devon Avenue was one of the reasons that we liked the neighborhood so much. It immediately became our shopping destination, including the Crawford Department Store, Lazar's, Parthenon Restaurant for the world's best gyros, Hobbymodels, and the Green River for Chinese food. Of course, Miller's Steak House at Lunt and Western was a very elegant spot and so close to our house that we usually didn't have to get a baby sitter when we went there."

Miller also likes living in the West Rogers Park neighborhood because of its religious and ethnic diversity. "The neighborhood today has many different groups with no dominant religious preference. Our nearest neighbor is Catholic and we see Christmas lights and decorations all around. On the Jewish holidays there are succots and candelabras for Chanukah. Hispanic families in the neighborhood gather on weekends in Warren Park. And, of course, there are many Indian and Pakistani families living in the neighborhood. I think that the diversity is a terrific thing and I notice that home values continue to increase because residents take good care of their properties. We view our neighborhood as exciting and stimulating and a wonderful cultural, spiritual and intellectual environment."

Tango lessons at Indian Boundary Park Field House, 1990.

View of Adams property from point at greenhouse near Devon, 1909. (Courtesy of the Metropolitan Water Reclamation District.)

Jack Marshall, interviewed in February 1928

From Ridge to Western was pretty fair land, but west of California there were swamps again. I have heard that this land way over west was a shallow lake in the spring. They used to catch fish there. We all owned land in Niles Center in the Big Woods in the early times because it was good timber and we needed firewood. We had four acres and our taxes used to be twelve cents a year. We would hitch up the horses and drive straight west from Ridge to the woods across the frozen prairie and swamps to get to our wood in the winter. There used to be thousands of wild pigeons flying over the prairie.

Walter Prigge, interviewed in March 1926

The people have come largely from Lincoln Park, Lake View, Uptown and the Rogers Park section, seeking homes where they can have more room and can raise children. The crowded apartment house conditions in the older districts make it hard to raise children and they have come to this section desiring to own their own single-family homes and to be free from the crowded apartment house life and conditions. The real estate promotion spirit is great in the area, and it is characteristic phenomena in all new rapidly developing areas on the outskirts of the city. So many areas seem to have had such rapid expansion in the last three or four years as we return to "normalcy" after the stoppage of building and growth due to World War I.

The new cooperative apartments at the Indian Boundary Park, Park Manor, Park Castle, etc., are selling at from $6,000 to $12,000 an apartment, and they are reported to be selling rapidly too. They are very splendid-appearing apartments with a fine setting right on the edge of the park, as though that were their front yard.

Most of the people have their own autos and depend on them much more than the streetcars for transportation. A recent survey by the Auto Club revealed that this section of the city had a larger percentage of autos per population than any other district in the city. In fact, there is said to be a movement afoot among some property owners to oppose all efforts to get rapid transportation into the area. Transportation to the Loop is either in their own autos or by the surface cars and elevated. Most of the people seem to go to the Uptown center for their amusement and a good deal of their shopping. Many of the men are claimed to be connected with small manufacturing plants in the general small factory district further south along Western and small factories for light industry, some in Ravenswood and further south. They drive to their work in cars. They are either employers, owners of the shops or headmen, not working men, although some of them may be.

Clarence Hess, retiree

My grandfather, Peter Endre, came to Chicago from Luxembourg in the late 1800s, and he bought the land that became Indian Boundary Park. He also built a home and greenhouses located just north of that area, and they were still standing after World War II. The land where all of the co-op apartment buildings were built around Indian Boundary Park belonged to my grandfather, and in those days, real estate developers came around and offered to buy the land from him. However, he never got paid for the land although they gave him notes for it. During the Depression, the developers went bankrupt and my grandfather was stuck with all the liens on the land.

Howard and Western, looking north, 1931. (Courtesy of the CTA.)

Children's garden club, Indian Boundary Park, 1938. (Courtesy of the Chicago Park District.)

Wolf in Indian Boundary Park Zoo, 1938. (Courtesy of the Chicago Park District.)

Craft class in Indian Boundary Park Field House, c.1940. (Courtesy of the Chicago Park District.)

Draft Board 77, 7127 N. Western Avenue, c.1945. Photograph by Henry Green. (Courtesy of the Chicago Historical Society, ICHi 32260.)

Nancy Bild Wolf, medical administrator

I remember that on Sunday, December 7, 1941, I was practicing my piano when my brother's friend, Johnny Sarkisian, called up and said that the Japanese had bombed Pearl Harbor. Nobody knew where Pearl Harbor was, but it was like, "Oh, my Lord!" During the War, we were quite conscious of being a Jewish family and that there were bad things happening to Jews in Europe. But it was still kind of remote to us. And, looking back, I remember getting pictures and letters from people in Europe who had our same last name. They had searched the phone book and were trying to get to America. But my family was struggling, and we didn't have that much, and we didn't really know if those people were really related to us. Who knows what happened to them, and it's very sad when I look back because we weren't able to do anything to help them.

Howard Fink, judge

I think that World War II was the central point in most people's lives. Relatives and neighbors had gone to fight the War, and, at school, War Stamps were important. At the age of six, around the time when Wake Island fell, I began to follow the War on a daily basis. I had a large map and I used little pins to mark places where there were important battles and events. As for rationing, I couldn't get any bubble gum, and candy was also being rationed. We weren't deprived of important things, but as kids we were very aware of the War. You knew that there was some difficulty getting meat. You also knew the problems with getting rubber and that everything was rationed. You knew that your mom was always going places with a ration book. We also were aware that there was black marketing going on, and people throughout the neighborhood frowned on such activities. There was very strong patriotism in the neighborhood.

Bert Sherman, attorney

I'll never forget the block party that we had on Sherwin Avenue after World War II; it was a block party to end all block parties. To me, it was the "cat's meow," because the party encompassed Sherwin Avenue, and went from Washtenaw to Sacramento, across California. I can remember that everyone was so happy that the War was over, and all I cared about was the free pop and free food. It was just a marvelous thing, and something I will always remember.

Checks for good work, Boone School, 1942. Photograph by Henry Green. (Courtesy of the Chicago Historical Society, ICHi 32272.)

Ice skaters from Boone School dance club, c.1945. Photograph by Henry Green. (Courtesy of the Chicago Historical Society, ICHi 25579.)

Candlelighting ceremony honoring the PTA, Boone School, c.1945. Photograph by Henry Green. (Courtesy of the Chicago Historical Society, ICHi 32263.)

Sidney Bild, physician

I went to Boone Grammar School during the 1930s. It was a good grammar school and the teachers were pretty tough. I think that there must have been fourty-eight seats in the classrooms, and most of them were filled as we moved up from class to class. I recall one of the exciting times, and it was a horrible thing that happened, when one of the proprietors of a school lunch store on Pratt was found murdered. There were two stores across from Boone: Mr. Brinkman and his wife ran one that sold primarily candy and ice cream; Mrs. Mable had lunches, including very good hot dogs. Most of the time we brought our own lunch to school and ate it wherever we could. It was during the Depression and spending money for lunch was not considered very cool. One morning, I went to the school store before school at about 8 a.m., and there were kids lined up to get in, but it was locked up. So we went to school, but during the day word filtered out that Mrs. Mable had been murdered.

Gary Berg, attorney

I went to Boone School in the 1940s. When I first went there, I was a crybaby, but as I got older I became big and strong, and larger than the other kids. So, I set up my own "protection" racket for kids on their walk to and from school. For many years, I was protecting one girl and we would stop at Cal-Lunt Pharmacy. Since they had a soda fountain there, she would have to buy me a milkshake when I wanted it. In grammar school, I was a bad kid, so the teachers treated me the worst. I remember a practice graduation event when Mrs. Nyhill, the assistant principal, decided that I was talking during the middle of the ceremony. She said that I had to write the phrase, "I will not talk in the assembly hall" a thousand times. So, I got up there and I wrote, "I will not talk in the assembly hall," and then I wrote down the number 1,000. She wasn't too happy with me.

Dan Miller, journalist

Our experience with Boone School was terrific. We had been concerned about the kind of education that our children would receive in the Chicago Public Schools, but the fact is that they learned everything that we would have wanted for their grammar school education, including reading and writing. Our principal at Boone School knew all our kids' names, their strengths and weaknesses and their reputations. We became active at Boone, and we would attend events and parent-teacher things. At the time that our kids were going there in the '70s and '80s, we were very pleased with our children's education.

Clay Pit, looking north from gas tank, c.1945. Photograph by Henry Green. (Courtesy of the Chicago Historical Society, ICHi 32280.)

Nancy Bild Wolf, medical administrator

In the 1930s, west of our house on the 2900 block of Fitch, there was the clay pit. We used to go tobogganing there. The nice thing was that the older children, especially my brother, Sidney, would supervise us. He would look over the area because there were a lot of trees and you could possibly hurt yourself. So we would seek a clear path, with the older kids telling us where to go. Some of the older ones would actually go to the bottom of the pit and watch us as we tobogganed. It was just delightful, and the clay pit was also a place to find wildflowers. But, my mother always told me that there might be some strangers down there, so, unlike my brother, I didn't go excavating or exploring in the pit. I went with him once when he climbed down to the deeper end, and I saw a spring running down the middle of it, as well as rushes and other flora. It was just fun to know that it existed.

Howard Fink, judge

During World War II, we would play at the clay pit because we lived at 2948 W. Estes, right next to it. We would look across the pit and, all during WW II, we became convinced that the Germans were coming. Ironically, we got that idea because people had told the neighborhood kids that the Germans were nearby. What we didn't know was that there was a partial truth to that claim, since there was a German P.O.W. camp in Glenview. And we would be waiting there to defend the country, and West Rogers Park, from the enemy with our BB guns and popguns.

Janet Zimmerman, on Op-Ed Page, *Chicago Sun-Times*, January 11, 1961

The property owners in the area bounding the Touhy Avenue "clay pit" have themselves to thank for their present difficulties. They had a beautiful, ready-made park ten years ago in this abandoned clay pit. Natural springs kept the deepest part of the pit filled with fresh water cattails and other marsh plants grew on the margins. The area was a bird sanctuary that attracted nature lovers from the entire Chicago region. It was listed in Olin Sewall Pettingill's *Guide To Bird Finding East of the Mississippi River*, published by Oxford Press in 1951. Red-winged blackbirds nested in the cattails and rails, coots and gallinules in the marshy edges. Several kinds of swallows and kingfishers skimmed the surface of the lake and, incidentally, kept down the mosquito population of the neighborhood. Black-crowned night herons fished there in the evenings, and occasionally osprey or fish eagles visited the pit. One spring a lovely snowy egret stayed there for some time. Along the east side, at the street level, was rose hedge that was bursting with warblers, goldfinches and other small birds, especially during the spring and fall migrations. The Illinois Audubon Society, the Chicago Ornithological Society and the Evanston Bird Club made every effort to save the clay pit. Members called on every property owner in the vicinity. They contacted the local weekly newspaper and civic organizations. They called on the Chicago Park Board and tried to interest the city in buying the property. We had complete plans for developing the park -- a high wire fence around the base of the pit to protect children; lawns and benches where people could sit and look out across it and watch the birds. We were met with total indifference from everyone. They still have no appreciation of what they threw away. It took ten years to fill in the pit, during which time they could enjoy a hideous eyesore. Now, if they don't have high-rise apartments, the best they can get is just one more ball field.

Phil Hodapp, in *The Historian*, Winter 1997-98

In 1928, while the Park Gables was still under construction, my parents came to Chicago where my father had accepted a professorship in sociology at Loyola University. Upon seeing the building on Estes Avenue north of Indian Boundary Park, my parents purchased an apartment at 2478-1. The unit was not finished so the newlyweds spent their first three months living in the party room.

Estes is blocked off at each end of our building, making it ideal for families. Children did not have to cross any streets to get to the park. Most of the time all the kids from the building were in the park or a nearby play area, so there was no time for a kid to be bored. Traffic on Fitch Avenue was not heavy. After a snowstorm, several of us would pull our sleds to the corner of Western and Fitch and grab on to the bumpers of the cars turning west. Nothing like a free ride. There were three hills we used for sledding in the winter, two behind the gas station on Touhy and one at the northeast corner of the duck pond which was used in winters for ice-skating. The Park District maintained the ice rink. Snow was removed and the rink was flooded with a new surface when needed. Skaters moved to music, courtesy of the owner of apartment 2460-1 who put speakers on his porch. After the Christmas holidays, we would collect dried out Christmas trees, stack them in the prairie on the west side of the building and then schedule the biggest bonfire we could imagine.

Hugh Downs, broadcaster

In 1952 and 1953, I was the announcer for the NBC Network TV program *Kukla, Fran & Ollie*. In addition to announcing, I also joined Fran Allison as another human element at the puppet stage. Burr Tillstrom, the show's creator and master puppeteer, had an incredibly compartmentalized mind. In the years that I watched him and worked with him, I never saw him make the error of crossing a voice. His characters, like humans, would on occasion make an error, but there was never confusion about which of his "people" were talking. One Sunday afternoon at the Actors' Club in Chicago, Burr set up his small portable stage for a brief presentation to the members. Prior to this production, we had all been drinking, and Burr joined in with the stoutest of those quaffing. He was noticeably on the way to inebriation. As a result, Ollie was not sober during the performance. But -- and this was spooky -- Kukla did not drink, and his authentic sobriety was impressive. He was exuding disapproval of Ollie's behavior. He was saying things like, "Don't come to me tomorrow with a throbbing head -- you'll get no sympathy from me!" I have never seen anything like it. Kukla was cold sober -- Burr Tillstrom was not! What kind of brain could hold off the effects of alcohol for one of its puppet characters and not the others? We were mystified. But those characters were very real to Burr Tillstrom and, as a result, they were extremely real to viewers and fans.

Scott Simon, broadcaster

I remember the time two of my friends from Senn were on a date and one night they got caught making out in the woods at Indian Boundary Park. Mind you, we were city kids and we did not trust the woods. It could only be something as powerful a force as adolescent lust that would drive us into the woods. So, in any event, they just happened to pick the one spot at Indian Boundary Park where a policeman was walking. As a result, the two of them had to come out "red-faced," adjusting their clothes and trying to look as innocent as possible. Of course, the cop said that he was going to call their parents. But the worst part of it was that my friend maintained that he was picking twigs out of his derriere for weeks. The whole incident proved to me that one should probably stay out of the woods, or city parks, at night.

Burr Tilstrom and Lynn Millaid's marionette group, Indian Boundary Park Field House, c.1940. (Courtesy of the Chicago Park District.)

Opening ceremonies for Rogers School addition, 1952. (Courtesy of the Chicago Park District.)

Ron Menaker, attorney

I went to Rogers Elementary School, and, when I started there in the late '40s, it was the original school that just ran north and south. There were no east and west wings to it. And, south from the school, which is now Rogers School Park, were all the Second World War veterans. They were living in mobile barracks that had been erected there. The whole park was full of them. I remember them as square rather than hut-shaped, and they weren't made of metal. They were square like trailers, but they were stationary, and they were white. When I started grammar school in 1948, a lot of kids who attended Rogers School were the sons and daughters of the veterans living in those trailers.

Michael Zelmar, attorney

When I started at Rogers in the '50s, it was on shifts, but the kids were no longer going to the portables. In third grade, I was on the afternoon shift and, in fourth grade, I was on the morning shift. By the time I was promoted to fifth grade, they had built the additions to Rogers. In fifth grade, we had three different teachers, including Ms. Patton and Ms. Pappas. They were just young women and probably beginning their first teaching jobs. Our classroom was located just above the principal's office. And, when there was commotion in the room, Dr. Elkin could hear us and probably realized that the young teachers were having a difficult time controlling the kids, so he would frequently be up in our room. I can still remember one time that he came storming into the classroom because we were making so much noise, had his say to us, and left after slamming the door. The act of slamming the door created enough of a wind current that it caused one of the paper airplanes stuck in the fluorescent lights to fall gently to the ground.

Bob Berman, farmer

One of my great moments living in West Rogers Park happened when I was about eleven years old. Our home was on Sherwin Avenue across the street from the Rogers School playground. In the winter, the Chicago Park District would freeze a portion of the park for an ice skating rink. A wooden, one-room structure was brought in and it had a coal-powered stove. My friends and I used to play hockey on the rink and then warm up in that little house. On one particular school night in the winter, I had finished my homework and was allowed to go across the street and ice skate. The rink was lit up by a bright park streetlight, and that night there was freezing rain that completely covered everything in the park, including the ice rink, the tennis courts, the basketball courts and the softball fields. Everything was frozen over like smooth glass, and I skated every inch of the park that night as if I was gliding on a river. There were only one or two other skaters experiencing that enchanting phenomenon that night, and it became a great memory for me.

Kids at Thillens Stadium, c.1950.

Ulcer Eliminator, Thillens Stadium, c.1950.

Mayor Richard J. Daley with Mel Thillens, Sr. at Thillens Stadium, c.1960.

Glenn Jacobs, bank executive

I went to Thillens Stadium a lot when I was growing up on Sacramento in the '60s. I played baseball there for a number of years on a Little League team and I loved it. I also remember that there was a great place called the Hot Dog Ranch that was located right near Thillens. I always used to look forward to getting a bag of French fries there because it was served in a brown paper bag with grease oozing from it.

Dan Miller, journalist

When I came to Chicago in the late '60s, we had no idea about the importance of Thillens Stadium. I started at the *Chicago Daily News* in December of 1968, and the next spring I met Mike Royko who, of course, was a very avid softball player. So we played in a league, and somehow or other we ended up playing at Thillens, and to me it was just that we were going to play softball in my neighborhood. Well, to all these other people, to play at Thillens was the height of neighborhood glory. I was so surprised that right here in my own neighborhood was Thillens Stadium.

Bruce Wolf, broadcaster

It was like a dream to be in a game at Thillens Stadium, and even as a suburban kid I wanted to play there. But, I never got a chance to actually play in a Little League game at Thillens because you had to win your own league championship to be able to play there. I had cousins who were in games there under the lights, but I was never fortunate enough to do that when I was younger. However, for a number of years, as sports editor at the Lerner Newspapers, I had to organize the Lerner baseball tournament and we would have it at Thillens Stadium. I mean, I was there for hours on end. Later, I wound up getting to play there in softball games against the Bears. Once, I almost busted my ankle against a guy who was a none-too-great running back for the Bears in an exhibition game at Thillens.

Scott Turow, author and attorney

In 1952, when I was three, we moved from an apartment at Arthur and Leavitt to a house my parents built on Sherwin, west of California. It was a wonderful neighborhood in which to grow up. I was, of course, under the illusion that everybody in the entire world was Jewish. I remember having a vigorous argument with Ina Schwartz about whether a black man who we saw on the corner of Touhy and California was Jewish, and I don't remember which side I was on, but I think I was on the Jewish side. It was unthinkable to me that everybody in the world wasn't Jewish. There was one Gentile fellow, John Larson, with whom we went to grade school, and, of course, there were the kids who went to St. Margaret Mary's. But, I don't know where they were, because they certainly weren't hanging around with me. Until I was thirteen or fourteen years old, I really never had friends who weren't Jewish.

I have to tell you that by the time I was that age, it struck me as an extremely peculiar way to be growing up. I can't say that I was wildly enthusiastic about it. I loved West Rogers Park. It had the sort of closeness of a shtetl and God knows how many synagogues there were. There literally seemed to be one every four square blocks. I always thought of our neighborhood as West Rogers Park. I don't know if there was some kind of social status attached to saying "West Rogers Park." There probably was, and I probably learned it from my mother, but it was the newer part of Rogers Park. I went to the Rogers School portables originally at Touhy and Sacramento, then I went to Decatur, and, ultimately, I went to Rogers and graduated there.

I attended New Trier High School because my parents decided to move. I started at New Trier while we were still living in West Rogers Park because my father had a coronary, which delayed our moving into the new house in Winnetka. And, I did really resent it when my parents moved, because I loved West Rogers Park so much. I went from a place where I had complete mobility as an older child, to a suburban environment where if your mother wouldn't drive you someplace, you were really stuck. So, it was not a happy transition as far as I was concerned. I didn't know anybody. The cliques that form in junior high school were impenetrable to me. I immediately began to experience subtle and eventually not so subtle anti-Semitism.

For me, the word I keep coming back to is intimacy. West Rogers Park was a wonderful place to grow up. Part of it was mobility as a child. The number of times I walked to Sandy's or Louie's for lunch from school was countless. And, it was safe, it was known, it was interesting. There were nice parks, good schools, and a community concerned about the community. I grew up on a wonderful block where both the parents and children are still interested in each other to this day. Certainly, a lot of the closest friendships I have developed over the years evolved from relationships with my Sherwin Avenue neighbors. I really thought it was the greatest thing in the world. For me, it was a wonderful, warm neighborhood and an intimate place to live and grow up, and that is what stands out.

Rogers School Park, c.1965. (Courtesy of the Chicago Park District.)

The North Town Neighborhood

Boundaries:
Bryn Mawr Avenue to Devon Avenue (S-N)
Western Avenue to North Shore Channel/Kedzie Avenue (E-W)

The North Town neighborhood in 1900 was mostly prairie and farmland with scattered springs and bogs. There were only a few residents, most of them working their land and living in farmhouses that were dispersed throughout the area. There were a few stores and businesses and some paved roads. Similar to West Rogers Park, it would not be until 1920 that any significant construction would begin on houses and two- and three-flat apartment buildings along with the slow, but steady development of Devon Avenue as a major commercial thoroughfare.

By 1932, when Joan Berets Tiersky moved there, the North Town neighborhood was maturing with houses and apartment buildings between Western and California, as well as stores on Devon. There was still considerable open space west towards Kedzie Avenue. "Our first apartment was at 6219 N. Washtenaw and we later moved to 6334 N. Talman. Most corner lots were empty and Devon was just beginning to be developed. Jewish shopkeepers began moving into the area in the late '30s. My grandfather was the founder of Congregation Ner Tamid on California and he would give Hebrew lessons to neighborhood boys preparing for their bar mitzvahs. When I first moved there, most of the people in our area were Swedish. There were very few Jewish families."

Tiersky attended Clinton Elementary School before going to Senn High School. "It was very difficult to get to Senn because there was no bus on Peterson at that time, so we would have to take the Devon bus to Clark and the streetcar to Peterson. I remember that my homeroom teacher was not very literate and had difficulty pronouncing words and when she would give us spelling tests, it was the most difficult thing in the world because we couldn't understand her."

Dorothy Dubrovsky Fields was sixteen years old when her family moved to 6238 N. Sacramento. "The neighborhood was very different than it is today. There were only a few Jewish families living near us in 1936. In fact, I remember seeing a sign on one of the apartment buildings that read, 'No Jews, No dogs, No children.' I was very sensitive about it because I had moved from a part of the northwest side that was very Jewish. Devon Avenue was the center of our lives. I recall such stores as Hillman's Stop-and-Shop, the Crawford Department Store, Kay Martin's, Cover Girl and Manzelmann Hardware Store."

There were two movie theaters in the neighborhood when Art Berman was growing up there in the 1940s. "The Cine was one of my favorite places to spend long afternoons watching movies, cartoons and serials. It was located on Devon and Maplewood and I used to go there whenever I didn't go to the Nortown on Western, south of Devon. The nice thing about those two theaters was that we could walk to them. As for shopping, there were good, solid retailers on Devon where my parents took me as a child and where I continued to shop as an adult. And I loved the Chinese food at Pekin House and Kow-Kow."

Howard Fink lived in West Rogers Park but visited the Cine and Nortown theaters on a regular basis. " Everybody went to the movies. The Cine was the cheap theater and featured 'B' movies. I can still remember going to see *Captain Marvel*, the serials and the cartoons there, but that theater closed sometime in the early '50s. The Nortown was the higher-priced theater and it carried regular feature runs. We would go there as teens either on Friday nights with friends or Saturday nights if we had dates. Except for boys and girls on dates, Saturday night at the Nortown seemed to be a time reserved for our parents to go to the movies."

Joseph Epstein remembers going to Green Briar Park on Peterson. "We used to play at Green Briar and Ed Kelly, who would become a major figure in Chicago politics, was the sports director there in the 1940s. He was a wonderful guy and great with the kids. I would ride my bicycle or walk to the park from our apartment on Campbell Avenue. Devon was one of my favorite streets because it was very grand. It was the 'Jewish Renaissance,' and there were stores like Seymour Paisin's Dress Shop and Hillman's Stop-and-Shop, an elegant place with the supermarket downstairs and the delicates-

Cine Theatre, c.1935.
(Courtesy of the Theatre
Historical Society of America.)

Rogers Park B'nai Brith honors Bob Berenson, 1946. Photograph by Henry Green.
(Courtesy of the Chicago Historical Society, ICHi 32273.)

sen and restaurant upstairs. I also remember Neissner's, Kresge's, Abram's and the Crawford Department Store. My favorite Chinese restaurant was the Pekin House whose Chinese owner began to look more Jewish as he grew older. For a while I worked as a busboy at Pekin House for $.70 an hour, and we could eat anything we wanted for free except the shrimp dishes because they were more expensive."

Janie Friedman Isackson spent her early years in the North Town neighborhood during the mid- to late-1940s. "I lived at 6037 N. Mozart which was near where they built Mather High School in 1959. The area behind us was prairie and we used to play in the empty lots. I remember Brusow's on the corner of Glenlake and California, the fire station on California at Rosemont, the Jewel near Green Briar Park, and Lad and Lassie Nursery and Kindergarten. I have nice memories about living in that neighborhood before I moved to West Rogers Park in 1949."

Ira Berkow arrived in the North Town neighborhood in 1953 from Chicago's West Side and lived at 6224 N. Mozart. He has memories of Devon Avenue, including "Randl's, the Red Hot Ranch and Bow-Wow. Bow-Wow was a small diner where they had great steak sandwiches. My friend, Jerry Snower, used to accuse me of always having my eyes closed when I was eating a steak sandwich there. I guess it was because I enjoyed it so much that it almost transported me to another world. Green Briar Park was also an important part of my life in the neighborhood because we used to play baseball and basketball there all the time."

During the 1950s and 1960s, Steve Friedman lived in the North Town neighborhood at 6133 N. Campbell. "It was a great neighborhood, and I can remember going with my father, every September, to 'Z' Frank Chevrolet and the Pontiac dealers on Western Avenue to look at new cars. And, of course, we would always go to Friedman's Delicatessen for their great corned beef sandwiches. The restaurant was next to the Nortown Theatre and it was the best deli in the neighborhood."

Carl LaMell and his family came to the North Town neighborhood in 1952 when he was seven years old and in second grade. He lived in a three-flat at 6229 N. Talman, and the neighborhood "looked pretty much like it is now, except for the empty lot on the corner of Rosemont and Talman where they built an apartment building, and an empty lot two doors north of me where they constructed a two-flat. We used to play line ball in the empty lots throughout the neighborhood. And we had this game called Rolevio that involved two teams of kids. You had to hide and the other kids had to catch you. If they caught you, they would put you in 'jail' and we had to sneak around and free people from jail. This meant that we were running around everybody's backyard and some of the parents would stand outside and yell at us to play somewhere else. But, we played that game every night after dinner in the summer."

In high school, LaMell and his friends had special hangouts they called the "box" and the "wall." "The 'box' was the Plexiglas enclosure where you could wait for the bus at Granville and California, in front of Zucker's

Girl Scouts at Green Briar Park Field House, 1945. Photograph by Henry Green. (Courtesy of the Chicago Historical Society, ICHi 32270.)

Devon at Artesian, 1955. Photograph by Merrill Palmer. (Courtesy of the Chicago Sun-Times.)

Pharmacy. It was a favorite meeting place for all of our friends during summer evenings. The 'wall' was literally a small wall at Granville and Francisco where we could goof around and meet with friends after our dates."

Linda Holdman Wine lived on the corner of Hood and Sacramento where she had moved in 1956 from Humboldt Park. "The North Town neighborhood seemed very upscale because there were people who lived in houses or two-flats. I remember spending a lot of time at the field house at Green Briar Park. We had our fortnightly dances there where we learned to dance, have good manners and wear white gloves. My girlfriends and I were very athletic and we played volleyball and softball at Green Briar. If you knew someone who belonged to the Tower Cabana on Peterson, you could use the swimming pool there. It was a private club and they also had ice-skating in the winter."

Cameron Dall remembers going to the Nortown in the 1960s. " I feel very fortunate that I was able to be a part of what I consider the end of the great era of movie palaces. I remember one time when my father dropped us off for a kids' matinee. We bought a box of Cracker Jack and a Hershey's chocolate bar and we watched cartoons and a movie. The Nortown was giving away a bicycle and we had to keep our stubs to see if we won. A few hours later my father came to pick us up and although the movie was still playing, they let him in to wait for us and even gave him a candy bar. He sat in the back of the theater until everything was over and then we walked home. Kids don't have that kind of experience today, and I look back on it as a great way to spend an afternoon in an air-conditioned movie palace."

Glenn Jacobs lived in the North Town neighborhood throughout his entire childhood on Sacramento, between Granville and Rosemont. In the 1960s, he attended Green Elementary School on Devon, between California and Sacramento from kindergarten through sixth grade, before going to Clinton Elementary and then to Mather High School. "I remember Green School and the places around there on Devon, including Rosen's Drugstore, Bow-Wow's for hot dogs, and Fan's Fishery, a Jewish delicatessen. My family would go there to buy smoked fish and corned beef and all that good stuff. Green School had a big playground with a basketball court where we used to play. Thillens Stadium was also close and I played Little League there for a number of years."

Once Mather opened in 1959, kids from the North Town neighborhood went there. Mitch Joseph lived at 6212 N. Whipple, went to Green and Clinton, and in 1976 he started at Mather. "I spent some of the greatest years of my life at Mather. I loved high school, played on a lot of sports teams, and was involved in many school activities, including being voted senior class president. The neighborhood was beginning to change with greater diversity of ethnic, racial and religious groups, but I thought it was good to be exposed to people from other cultures. Although there was alcohol and drug use in my high school in the '70s, it was an individual choice and didn't really affect my life there. I look back on my years in the neighborhood with positive memories. The schools were

Mather High School, 5835 N. Lincoln, 1961. Photograph by Hedrich-Blessing.
(Courtesy of the Chicago Historical Society, HB-22899.)

Devon and Western, 1962. (Courtesy of the CTA.)

good, and family and community life was good in the North Town neighborhood."

Bruce Wolf was born on the West Side of Chicago and grew up in Skokie, but often visited his grandmother who lived near Devon and California. "She lived next to where the North Town Library was opened north of Devon, on California. My grandmother had an apartment on the third floor and it was weird, scary, and kind of uncomfortable for a suburban boy to have to climb those gray, back stairways and porches. I remember the little red wagon that my grandmother used when she went shopping on Devon to get the Cott Cola that we would drink for Passover.

"My memories of Devon Avenue include Ruby's Red Hots, owned and operated by Arnie and Estelle Hoffman, friends of my parents. There was Randl's at Devon and California and Pekin House, east of Western. I remember taking a date there in high school and the bill was $6. For some reason I gave a $2 tip. Maybe I just wanted to impress my date. In addition, I spent a lot of time in the North Town neighborhood over the years when I was the sports editor for the Lerner Newspapers."

Abdulaziz Daya was born in Karachi, Pakistan, in 1952, and immigrated to the United States in 1978, first living in Albany Park before moving with his family to the neighborhood in the mid 1980s. "I don't think of the neighborhood as Rogers Park, but rather as our Pakistani community. When I moved in, only a few Pakistanis were living around us. But more of my people began to move there. I think that the neighborhood is special for many reasons, but primarily because it is close to my work, there are plenty of places to shop and eat, and we also feel safe here. It really feels like a community."

Rick Kogan sees something very special about Rogers Park and West Ridge. "The two communities and their numerous neighborhoods have been extremely hospitable and nurturing to the various waves of immigrants over the past 170 years. They are neighborhoods where the 'soil' has made them into very organic communities where people can put down roots, open small storefront businesses, and become integral parts of the neighborhoods. Diversity is one way to describe the neighborhoods, but they have almost been like 'Phoenixes' rising from the ashes each time new groups arrive and the communities respond by redefining themselves. I think that a research project focusing on the social and cultural changes in Rogers Park and West Ridge over the past fifty years would be a great topic for an urban historian."

Devon Avenue shopkeepers Annie and Ram Dixit, 1992.

Four views of Devon and Western, 1914. (Courtesy of the CTA.)

Catherine Lulling, interviewed in April 1926

My father worked in Chicago as a plasterer for four years and then due to my mother's severe illness they decided to move out of the city and take up truck farming. Thus the family came to the area around the present West Rogers Park, our home standing until the last three or four years at the corner of what is now Devon and Western. My father's farm extended from Peterson to Devon and from Campbell to Western. This section was farmed at that time, what few farmers there were, by Germans and Luxembourgers. I recall no Irish, English or people of other nationalities in the section in the early days for the Luxembourg element seemed to predominate, but it was impossible to differentiate. The Luxembourg language is a dialect of German so that all of us associated with practically no difference many of the Germans speaking Luxembourg. We bought our farm from an agent who had gotten it directly from the government. The land had never been cultivated but was virgin prairie that had to be broken and plowed. Rogers Park to the lake was farming land and west as far as we could see was prairie and brush. Birds were plentiful in those days and there were many different kinds. The roads were few and in poor shape. There were also small Luxembourg centers or colonies in Niles and Evanston, and in the South Chicago section. All the Luxembourgers in the section have been in this country and in this area for thirty or forty years. The earliest neighbors we had lived over by Peterson Avenue past Lincoln Avenue. They were two farmers, Mr. Turner and Mr. Chistler. After a bit, Mr. Houvley, the postmaster, settled on Rosehill Avenue near Peterson. And then the Trumpellers moved here, near to where the Orphanage is now.

One day my father said to my mother, "I wish I could find the owner of the land across the road," as he pointed to the tract that now lies between Peterson, Devon, Western and California. On the very next day the owner came out and my father asked him about the rental. The owner, however, wanted to sell and suggested that my father get a few of the neighbors together and each buy a portion. This was done and the land was sold for $25 an acre. My father paid $28 for his land because it was a little nearer gravel deposits. In this whole plot not a foot of ground was open; it was prairie. Toward the east, the land was inclined to be sandy; in the center it was covered with good fresh water springs and at the west end was clay. People who see the fine lawns today do not realize the task it was to make anything grow on that land sixty years ago. My father dug little ditches and made little drains on the land where the springs were and drained the water. Then this made good farmland. To the south we had to plant corn and let it rot on the ground and the next year we could cultivate this soil. I have dug out the roots of more than one tree myself in order to make the land plowable.

But with all our hard work we had our pleasures too. On Sundays we would be at a neighbor's house for dinner. All the neighbors would be there. We would have a nice lunch and afterwards the young folks would dance and the men play cards. When night came we went home happy and gay. It was neighborly entertainment and although our pleasures were simple, we had a better time than the young folks today. The dances and parties given by the Devon-Western Business and Improvement Association often remind me of our parties when I was a girl.

Mr. Becker, interviewed in February 1928

I was born here in 1861. My father owned a farm from the alley west of the Northwestern tracks to Robey Street (now Damen Avenue) and from Peterson to Winandy's land on our north. He had a truck garden when I was a boy. It was all wilderness here when my father came. He worked hard and so did we kids. My children laugh at me now when I say they don't work. They won't do the things I did; it's a waste of energy to them. But no one came here with money from the old country. They had their health and were willing to work hard. It was no place for people who couldn't or wouldn't work. I don't know why the people came out here. They could buy lots for $2 in the city then, but they came here anyway. I guess someone started in here and the others followed. It took long enough to get to town, about three hours with a horse and wagon. But there was no use taking things that far at first, there was enough to do to get the land in shape to grow things and then raise them. The main thing was to get enough to eat. The trees had to be cleared in some parts too. We all worked. When I was five years old, I went along to help with the work and was expected to do as much as I could just like the men.

Devon and Western, looking north, 1931. (Courtesy of the CTA.)

March of Dimes display, Crawford Department Store, c.1940. Photograph by Henry Green. (Courtesy of the Chicago Historical Society, ICHi 32286.)

North Town Library patrons, c.1940. Photograph by Henry Green. (Courtesy of the Chicago Historical Society, ICHi 32256.)

North Town Library after-school program, c.1940. Photograph by Leonard Hart.

Story hour, North Town Library, c.1940. Photograph by Henry Green. (Courtesy of the Chicago Historical Society, ICHi 25610.)

Dorothy Dubrovsky Fields, retiree

We moved to Sacramento, near Devon, in 1936. There was a negative reaction by some of the area residents to the influx of Jewish families, and I remember being very sensitive to that treatment and such signs on apartment buildings as "No Jews, No Dogs." Despite this we rented an apartment in a three-flat, and after World War II, we built a two-flat at Sacramento near Peterson. Devon Avenue was really developing in the '30s and '40s, and a lot of Jewish families were moving into the neighborhood from Albany Park and the Northwest side of Chicago. I remember being on a streetcar with two ladies sitting in front of me. When we passed the Crawford Department Store on Devon, one lady said to her friend, "There are so many people moving into this neighborhood that shouldn't be moving here." I couldn't keep my mouth shut, and I said to her, "Did your mother and father come over on the Mayflower?" In fact, there was even a negative reaction by some of the Jewish residents in West Rogers Park to the newer, Eastern European Jews who were moving in.

Joan Berets Tiersky, retiree

In the 1930s and 1940s, Devon Avenue, and the neighborhood around it, was like a small town. Everybody knew everybody, and my family was very well-known in the area. My grandfather was a founder of Ner Tamid and my uncles, who helped to found the B'nai Brith on Devon above the Cine Theatre, were in local politics. One of my uncles, Milton Miller, was a precinct captain and also ran for alderman. I can remember places like the Town Pump on Western, south of Devon, and of course the Crawford Department Store, Abrams and Kay Martin's.

Gena Martinez Zelenka, librarian

I worked on Devon Avenue when it was totally Jewish. That was my first experience with Holocaust survivors. I worked with older people in a candy shop, and there was a woman there who had the numbers tattooed on her arm. I asked her about them and she told me about her experiences in the concentration camps during World War II. I saw a few other people during the summer of 1971 when I took buses to Devon Avenue that also were camp survivors. That made a strong impression on me because I realized that the Holocaust was true and that it had really happened. Before that, it was just an idea. But when I saw the tattoos, I realized that the Nazis had really done that to people and it made it real for me.

North Town Kiwanis Club at St. Mark's Church, 1944. Photograph by Henry Green. (Courtesy of the Chicago Historical Society, ICHi 32268.)

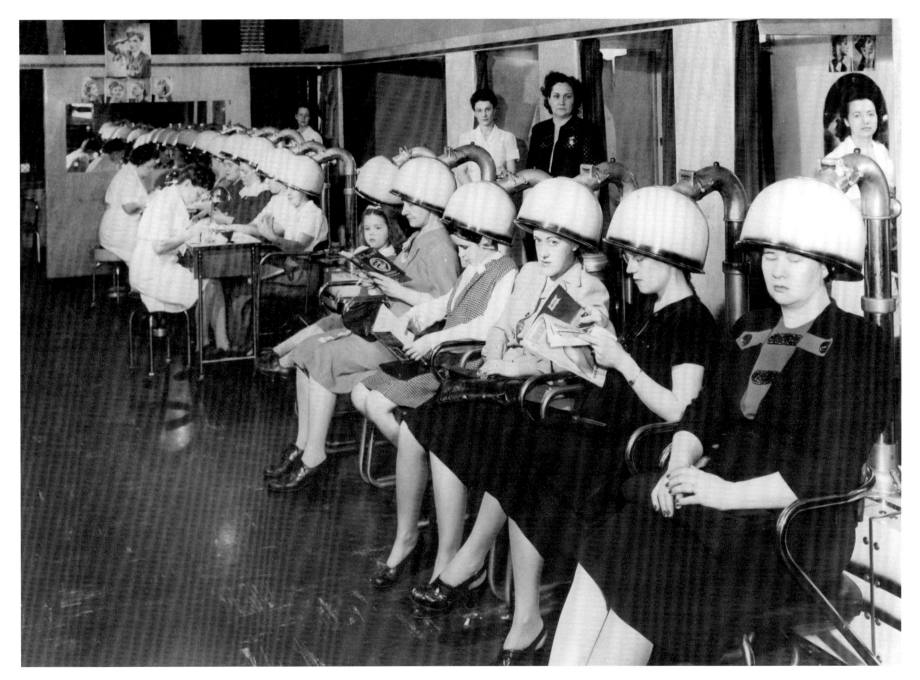

Millie's Beauty Salon, 6310 N. Western, c.1945. Photograph by Henry Green. (Courtesy of the Chicago Historical Society, ICHi 25611.)

Jump Meyers performs at Green Briar Park Field House, c.1950. Photograph by Henry Green. (Courtesy of the Chicago Historical Society, ICHi 25609.)

Student dance at Green Briar Park Field House, c.1950. Photograph by Henry Green. (Courtesy of the Chicago Historical Society, ICHi 16962.)

Looking east on Devon, c.1960. (Courtesy of the CTA.)

Linda Holdman Wine, business owner

In the 1950s and 1960s, Devon was our social hangout. We would walk the street and have certain stops. For example, there was Crawford's Department Store if we wanted to buy clothes, there was Bow-Wow Restaurant, which was just east of Sacramento, and there was Red Hot Ranch and Little Louie's Hot Dogs. My family went to Kow-Kow, a very popular Chinese restaurant. One of my cousins, who was about five years older and whom I considered to be a delinquent, used to hang out in front of Kofield's on the northeast corner of California and Devon. If you weren't a delinquent, you hung out on the southwest corner, at Randl's. As for shopping, there was Carol Korr, a very popular place to buy clothes. There was Manzelmann Hardware Store, and further east on Devon was Kenmac Radio Center where we spent a lot of time listening to records. It was great because it was the first place I remember where you could actually take a record, go into a booth, and listen to it.

Carl LaMell, special education school administrator

Devon was THE place in the neighborhood. We used to walk there every Saturday. It was our hangout and we would walk from Francisco to Western. We ate at Ruby's, the hot dog stand on Rockwell and Devon. Another group of kids in the '50s and '60s lived north of California and Devon and they would eat at Louie's. Those who lived west of California ate at the Ranch. When more of us started driving, we all ate at the Hot Dog Ranch. And, of course, there was Crawford's, Abrams, Manzelmann, Randl's and Kofield's. Randl's was the "in" place, but it was also the rough spot. There were fights there often, but people would hang out on that corner every weekend.

Susan Rosenberg RoAne, author and speaker

We always shopped on Devon in the '50s and '60s. My father used to say, "You don't need a Marshall Field's credit card. We have merchants from our own community and I don't care if we pay the extra $2 because we need to support local businesses." Those merchants included Carol Korr, Manzelmann, Stacy's Purse Store, Powder Puff Beauty Salon, and Crawford's Department Store. As for the restaurants, our favorites were Randl's, Kofield's, and Kow-Kow. You were either a Pekin House Chinese food person or a Kow-Kow Chinese food person, and we ate at Kow-Kow's all the time.

Nortown Theatre auditorium, c.1940. (Courtesy of the Chicago Sun-Times.)

Carl LaMell, special education administrator

I was thrown out of the Nortown Theatre forever. I have no idea what I did, but whatever it was it was bad enough to have a lifetime ban from that movie theater. In fact, one day, I showed up there on a date when I was eighteen, and the manager saw me, and he said, "You're not welcome here, still!" I also remember George's Popcorn that was next door to the Nortown, just south of the theater. It was the greatest place and they had candied apples and popcorn and candy that you could buy and take into the movie house.

Then, there was Friedman's Delicatessen that was north of the Nortown. Across Western Avenue, there was Robert's Deli, and, at the corner of Devon and Western, and there was Hobbymodels, on the northeast corner; General Camera on the northwest corner; and a restaurant on the southeast corner. On the east side of Western, across from the Nortown was the Town Pump and Sally's Ribs took its place later on. North of Devon and Western were Pike's Peak and Papa Milano's. The whole area around Devon and Western was just a wonderful, lively place when I was growing up in the '50s.

Mark Friedman, son of delicatessen co-owner

No history of Rogers Park/West Ridge would be complete without mentioning one particular restaurant that was a Western Avenue fixture for nearly thirty years, from the late 1940s until the mid-'70s. That restaurant was Friedman's Restaurant and Delicatessen, which was adjacent to the Nortown Theatre. My father was Oscar, one of the brothers who owned and operated that legendary place. Friedman's was well-known for serving up the best corned beef sandwiches and chocolate phosphates the city has ever known. It served those working and living in the area, the notable as well as the everyday person, and it was open around the clock. Many also made pilgrimages from all over the city to get a bowl of their cabbage, barley or chicken soups. During the years it occupied its place on Western, one of its neighboring businesses was a nightclub called the Rag Doll. During its heyday, the club featured such performers as Ella Fitzgerald, Nat "King" Cole and Dorothy Collins. Friedman's corned beef was also well-known by members of the World Champion New York Yankees in the late-fifties through the mid-sixties. It was all due to my father's friendship with the Yankee second baseman, Bobby Richardson. Every time Bobby came to Chicago with the team to play the White Sox, my father managed to bring a corned beef sandwich to Bobby. My father would take my mother, sister and me to the games, and would bring along a sack of sandwiches and kosher dill pickles for the guys, including Tony Kubek, Yogi Berra, Elston Howard and Whitey Ford.

Bruce Wolf, broadcaster

In 1961, the Blackhawks were in the Stanley Cup and, since they didn't televise their home playoff games, they would sell seats at Chicago area movie theaters for closed circuit showings of the games. One time, I remember going to the Nortown to watch the game. There were a couple of hundred people in the theater and it was jam-packed and people would stand to sing the national anthem. You're not at the stadium, and yet, people are acting as if they are there. So, it was kind of funny, and the noise was so loud in that theater, and there we are, watching a Stanley Cup hockey game with Bobby Hull and Stan Mikita. I don't think I have ever been at any sports event that was more exciting than that. Just being there, as a kid, with the loud noise and just watching the big screen, it was unbelievable.

Site for Mather High School and Park, looking south from Peterson, c.1950. (Courtesy of the Chicago Park District.)

Mather High School, main hallway, c.1960. Photograph by Hedrich-Blessing. (Courtesy of the Chicago Historical Society, HB 22899-M.)

Mather High School boy's gym class, c.1960. Photograph by Hedrich-Blessing. (Courtesy of the Chicago Historical Society, HB 22899-J.)

Linda Holdman Wine, business owner

Mather was wonderful and we were the first four-year class there in 1959. But it was crowded, and we had to have one-way halls because they could not accommodate everybody. If your locker was located on the corner, you would walk backwards so you wouldn't have to go all the way around. They had hall guards who were very strict, and, actually, one-way signs just as if you were on a street. I loved going to Mather, although not everybody has a positive memory of high school. I had a great time. I was on the volleyball team for a while, and I was active in theater, drama and music. Many of the teachers were quite young and it was their first teaching assignment, and, in fact, Mayor Daley's sister was an English teacher at Mather when it opened. The big social event was actually from Senn High School and it was the "Mert Davis" dance. We would go "canning" to raise money for the dance as part of our community service. The dance was called "Raven's Sweetheart," and it was at one of the big downtown hotels. Also, our club would have mixers with kids from other clubs and other high schools. The general feeling seemed to be that Mather had very stuck-up and snooty kids. There was the view that our football team never won a game because the boys on the team were too focused on how they looked, and that they would comb their hair before they put on their football helmets.

Steve Friedman, television producer

I started at Mather in 1960 and it was a giant place and brand new, especially coming from Clinton that was a smaller building and forty years old. So, we went from this old, dilapidated dump to this brand new high school and, rather than revel in this brand new place, we tried to turn it into a dump. It was just too nice for us, so we did everything we could to dirty it up. We ignored all those rules about walking in the one-way halls. We had a lot of great teachers at Mather, and there were a lot of people who we admired. The best looking teacher was Dawn McKee, a history teacher. A lot of guys went to her class, as opposed to the rest of them that we cut. Mr. Radziki taught math and he was a pretty good guy. I had Pat Daley, Mayor Daley's sister, for English, and the first time I met the mayor, she had taken us downtown to see the play, *The Miracle Worker*. Afterwards, we went into the Mayor's Office at City Hall. I was also in sports at Mather and I played baseball and football. Since we were a new school, it was hard to get a team together. But, we were in the worst division, the Blue Division, and we always played Sullivan.

Mitch Joseph, businessman

I went to Mather from 1976 to 1980 and it was probably the greatest four years of my life. I loved high school and I played on a lot of sport teams there. Socially, I was involved in everything from music to politics, and I was senior class president. When I was at Mather, there was a definite issue of drugs and alcohol, but I don't know if it was any different than previous years. For me, it was never really an issue, although there was always the "burn-out" crowd who were doing drugs outside school all the time. As far as favorite teachers at Mather, there was Tom Radziki who was the baseball coach and taught computer sciences. He was known as T.R. and he was definitely a hyper, strong guy who was optimistic, upbeat, and energetic, a real "Charlie-hustle" kind of person. He also ran the Adventures Club, which was a ski club. A lot of people joined that club just for the day ski trips. As far as music teachers, there was Mr. Hirsch, the orchestra director, and Mr. Olivo, the bandleader. I played trumpet and I was in All-City Band. I actually traveled to Europe with a band from the United States. At Mather, we had a phenomenal orchestra. My homeroom teacher was Ms. Reagan who taught Advanced Placement History. She had a great head on her shoulders and I had a lot of respect for her. And, another outstanding person at Mather was Burl Covan who was assistant principal and who directed the senior class. The man was a gem, a real mensch and a very nice guy. Mather was just a great school when I was going there.

Looking west on Devon, 1976. (Courtesy of the CTA.)

Devon Avenue bank sign, 1978. (Courtesy of the Chicago Sun-Times.)

Steve Friedman, television producer

I have very positive memories of Devon. Crawford's Department Store was a favorite place for my family to shop. I recall that Abrams was the place where I bought Boy Scout shoes and the shoe salesman would measure my feet while in the fluoroscope. When my friends and I went to Devon on Saturdays we would eat at Ruby's Red Hots, or walk to Friedman's on Western for a corned beef sandwich. We also ate at the Hot Dog Ranch near Thillens Stadium. Randl's and Kofield's were the two popular restaurants at the corner of Devon and California where all the kids would hang out on Saturday nights. Our neighborhood was clearly defined with its borders being Peterson, Devon, Western and California.

Dan Miller, journalist

One of the reasons that we like living in West Rogers Park is the closeness of Devon Avenue. It is our primary destination for shopping. We still have several of the items that we purchased at the Crawford Department Store, including furniture and jewelry. As for restaurants, we went to the Parthenon Restaurant because they made the world's best gyros. In the summertime, we would take the tomatoes from our garden and swap them at the Parthenon for gyro sandwiches. When the Hobbymodels was open at Devon and Western we used to go there to buy balsa wood for our kids to use in their arts and crafts classes at Indian Boundary Park.

Abdulaziz Daya, computer specialist

I came to the United States from Pakistan in 1978, and after living in Albany Park, we moved to the neighborhood. My family likes living near Devon because it is a very nice area, with a good mixture of Pakistani and Indian people. The only time when there has been tension between the two groups was when there were problems in South Asia. For a while, there were a lot of gang activities around us, but things have improved and we feel safe living there. My kids went to grammar school at Boone and Stone Academy, and high school at Lincoln Park High School in the International Baccalaureate program and Whitney Young High School. We like the area because the transportation is very good and we feel as if we are in the center of the city. We go to restaurants on Devon and do most of our daily shopping at the stores there.

Sari shop on Devon, 1984.

Subject Index

Photograph Index

Interview Index

Sources

Documents

Palmer, Vivien M. (ed.). *History of the Rogers Park Community, Chicago*. Prepared for The Chicago Historical Society and the Local Community Research Committee, University of Chicago, 1927.

Palmer, Vivien M. (ed.). *History of the West Rogers Park Community, Chicago*. Prepared for The Chicago Historical Society and the Local Community Research Committee, University of Chicago, 1927.

Newspapers and Journals

Chicago Daily News
Chicago History
Chicago Sun-Times
Chicago Tribune
Historian, The
Howard News, The
Lerner News
Loyola News
North Shore News
North Town News
Rogers Park Historical Society Newsletter
Rogers Park News
Rogers Park News Herald

Authors' Notes

There were three separate sources for the interviews quoted in this book. First, some of the interviews were gathered from residents who lived in the two neighborhoods during the late 1920s. These were conducted by the Local Community Research Committee of the University of Chicago as cited in the *History of the Rogers Park Community, Chicago* and the *History of the West Rogers Park Community, Chicago*. Second, there were several individuals who were interviewed by volunteers of the Rogers Park/West Ridge Historical Society from the 1970s through the 1990s and who are quoted in this publication. And third, most of the quotes were taken from more than one hundred interviews compiled by the book's coauthor, Neal Samors, throughout 2001. The Interview Index provides a complete listing of all individuals who have been quoted in this publication.

The Rogers Park/West Ridge Historical Society was founded in July of 1975 to gather and preserve the history of our two communities. Our collection currently consists of over 7,000 photographs dating to the 1870s and many other local memorabilia. Since 1985, an annual fall house tour has been conducted to showcase our unique architecture and the preservation of local residences. Our award-winning newsletter debuted in the spring of 1986 and is our primary means of communication with current and potential members. In 1991 we moved to our current location which houses our museum and educational research center. In October of 2000, the Society published its first book, *Chicago's Far North Side: An Illustrated History of Rogers Park and West Ridge*.

Student dance at Mundelein College, 1938. (Courtesy of Mundelein College, Women and Leadership Archives.)

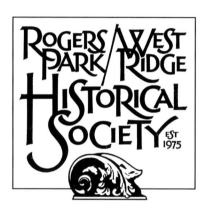